Advanced Svelte

Master Real-World Techniques for Building Reactive, Scalable Web Applications with Ease

Kevin Stolz

Table of Contents

3

Preface

This book was created to equip developers with the advanced skills necessary to build real-world, production-grade applications using Svelte. It goes beyond introductory tutorials and surface-level explanations. Instead, it focuses on the deeper patterns, architectures, and techniques that developers rely on when applications need to scale, perform efficiently, and remain maintainable over time.

At the center of this book is the understanding that Svelte is not just another UI framework. It represents a shift in how we think about building web applications — one where much of the heavy work is done during the build process rather than in the browser at runtime. By embracing this compilation-first philosophy, developers can create faster, smaller, and more responsive applications.

Throughout the book, you will explore how the Svelte compiler works under the hood, how reactivity can be managed cleanly even in complex scenarios, how to structure scalable codebases, and how to optimize your applications for both performance and accessibility. You will also see how to handle asynchronous operations, test applications rigorously, and prepare projects for real-world deployment challenges.

The examples and practices presented are grounded in real development experience. This ensures that what you learn here can be applied immediately to client projects, startups, enterprise systems, and everything in between.

This book is not about learning Svelte from scratch. It is about mastering Svelte when you are ready to build serious applications that need to stand the test of time, traffic, and technical complexity.

Who Should Read This Book

This book is designed for developers who already have a basic understanding of Svelte and who want to move beyond small applications and tutorials into real production work. If you are comfortable with concepts like components, props, reactive statements, and stores, you are ready for what is covered here.

You might be a front-end developer aiming to level up your skills to handle larger and more complex applications. You might be a software architect or team lead preparing to introduce Svelte into an organization and looking for best practices for scalability and maintainability. Or you might be a passionate builder who wants to push beyond the basics and use Svelte as the foundation for fast, reliable, and professional-grade web applications.

Although previous experience with frameworks like React, Vue, or Angular can be helpful, it is not required. What matters most is that you are willing to engage with more advanced techniques and design considerations that go into building serious applications.

The book is also valuable for developers transitioning from a basic understanding of SvelteKit to mastering full-scale application development, as many real-world examples and practices are aligned with how SvelteKit structures modern web projects.

How to Use This Book

The structure of this book is designed to allow you to either read it cover-to-cover or focus on specific chapters that are most relevant to your needs at a given time.

If you want a systematic mastery of advanced Svelte development, starting from Chapter 1 and progressing through the entire book will build your skills progressively. Each chapter builds on the concepts introduced in the previous ones, moving from compiler theory and reactivity patterns to real-world application architecture, performance optimization, and deployment readiness.

However, if you are working on a project and need immediate solutions, you can easily use individual chapters as references. For example, if you are dealing with asynchronous data handling issues, you can go directly to the chapter on asynchronous workflows. If you are focused on improving load times and responsiveness, you can jump to the performance optimization chapter without needing to read the earlier material first.

Code examples are provided throughout to illustrate key concepts. These examples are intentionally practical rather than theoretical. Wherever necessary, explanations accompany the code to show not just *what* to do, but *why* it is being done in a particular way, helping you make informed decisions in your own projects.

You are encouraged to experiment with the ideas presented, adapt the patterns to fit your specific applications, and think critically about the architectural choices you make as your applications grow. Mastery does not come from memorizing patterns but from understanding when and why to apply them.

While this book covers many cutting-edge practices, it is written to be future-conscious. That means where upcoming changes in the Svelte ecosystem — such as the introduction of Svelte 5 features — are relevant, they are discussed in context to help you future-proof your skills and projects.

Above all, use this book as a working companion to your development practice. The goal is not only to make you proficient in advanced Svelte but to make you confident in applying these skills across a wide variety of real-world challenges.

Chapter 1: Understanding the Svelte Compiler

When people first encounter Svelte, one of the most common impressions is how little code is required to produce something interactive. You write what looks like plain HTML, CSS, and JavaScript, and Svelte takes care of turning it into something efficient and reactive. But what really happens behind the scenes?

Unlike frameworks like React or Vue, which send a virtual DOM engine into the browser, Svelte does most of the work at build time. That's the heart of Svelte's power: **the compiler**. Understanding how the compiler works is crucial if you want to master Svelte at an advanced level. It gives you insight into why your code behaves a certain way, how to structure it for performance, and how to avoid hidden pitfalls that can creep in as your applications grow.

How Compilation Powers Svelte's Reactivity

When you first start writing Svelte components, it can feel like the reactivity is almost magical. You declare variables, bind them to the UI, and when the data changes, the interface updates automatically. But in truth, there is nothing magical happening. Svelte's reactivity is powered by something concrete, something you can understand and use to your advantage: **the compiler**.

Svelte is not like traditional JavaScript frameworks. Libraries like React and Vue rely on a virtual DOM — an in-memory representation of the real DOM — to determine what needs to be updated when data changes. They run a constant cycle of diffing and patching to keep the interface in sync with the application state. This process, while effective, always introduces some runtime overhead. The browser needs to do more work after your code loads, and that cost grows as your application grows.

Svelte approaches this fundamental challenge differently. Instead of running a virtual DOM engine in the browser, Svelte **moves the heavy lifting to the build step**. The Svelte compiler analyzes your code at build time and generates JavaScript that knows exactly how to update the DOM when changes occur. It doesn't need to figure out what to change after the fact; it already knows.

Let's take a simple example to really understand this.

Suppose you write the following component:

```svelte
<script>
    let count = 0;

    function increment() {
        count += 1;
    }
</script>

<button on:click={increment}>
    Count is {count}
</button>
```

When you see this, you might expect that every time you click the button, Svelte somehow *detects* that count has changed and then re-renders the button content. That would be the traditional way many frameworks operate.

But what Svelte actually does is different. At build time, the compiler transforms this code into highly optimized JavaScript. It generates instructions that:

Directly attach the click event listener to the button

Update the count value when increment() is called

Specifically change the **text content** inside the button after count changes, without touching anything else in the DOM

Here's a conceptual view of what the compiled JavaScript might resemble (simplified):

```javascript
const button = document.createElement('button');
button.textContent = `Count is ${count}`;
button.addEventListener('click', () => {
    count += 1;
    button.textContent = `Count is ${count}`;
});
```

Notice that there's no virtual DOM here. There's no re-rendering of the component. There's no reconciliation step. Svelte gives the browser direct,

9

imperative instructions to update exactly what needs updating — and nothing more.

This leads to several important consequences for real-world application development:

First, because updates are specific and targeted, **Svelte applications are naturally faster** than many virtual DOM-based applications, especially when dealing with frequent updates or large numbers of DOM elements.

Second, because everything is known at compile time, **there's less runtime overhead**. The browser is not burdened with maintaining a complex internal structure to track changes. It simply follows the direct update instructions that were generated ahead of time.

Third, your **bundle sizes are smaller** because you are not shipping a heavy framework runtime alongside your application logic. You ship your application logic alone, along with only the small helpers Svelte generates when needed.

Now, let's look at a slightly more complex real-world example to reinforce this concept.

Suppose you have a list of items that can grow when a user clicks a button:

```
<script>
    let items = ['Apple', 'Banana'];

    function addItem() {
        items = [...items, `Item ${items.length +
1}`];
    }
</script>

<ul>
    {#each items as item}
        <li>{item}</li>
    {/each}
</ul>

<button on:click={addItem}>
    Add Item
```

```
</button>
```

At build time, Svelte analyzes the `{#each}` block and generates efficient JavaScript to manage the `<ul>` and `<li>` elements. It doesn't re-render the entire list when `items` changes. It knows how to surgically update the DOM:

If a new item is added, Svelte generates code to create a new `<li>` element and append it to the `<ul>`.

If an item were removed, Svelte would generate code to remove the corresponding `<li>`.

If items are reordered, Svelte would update their positions directly without re-creating elements from scratch.

Again, no virtual DOM comparison. No guessing. Purely targeted updates based on compile-time knowledge.

This compilation strategy also means that **how you write your code affects what the compiler generates**. For instance, when you reassign the entire `items` array with `items = [...items, newItem]`, you are clearly signaling to Svelte that the `items` variable has changed. This triggers the DOM update instructions for the list. But if you were to mutate the array in place (for example, `items.push(newItem)` without reassigning), the compiler would have no way to detect that anything changed, because no reassignment occurred. In Svelte, reassignment is the trigger for reactive updates.

Understanding this relationship — between the way you write Svelte code and the way the compiler generates DOM update instructions — is key to mastering Svelte development.

In large-scale applications, where hundreds of components interact and many things change at once, this direct, compiled approach avoids the kinds of bottlenecks that virtual DOM frameworks often struggle with. You get performance that scales naturally, without needing to add complex memoization, manual DOM manipulation, or other optimizations.

As your applications grow, this compiler-first model becomes not just a performance advantage, but also an architectural advantage. Your code remains declarative and easy to reason about, while the compiler takes care of optimizing the imperative steps behind the scenes.

Hidden Optimizations and Performance Impacts

When you write Svelte code, it feels natural to think that the simplicity you see is what gets shipped to the browser. You declare some variables, write a few reactive statements, and Svelte makes the interface respond beautifully. But underneath the surface, the Svelte compiler is doing far more work than you might realize. It is actively rewriting and optimizing your code to make it as fast and as efficient as possible.

Many of these optimizations happen without you having to explicitly ask for them. However, knowing what the compiler does behind the scenes — and what it expects from you — can significantly impact the quality, speed, and scalability of the applications you build. Let's take a full, clear look at these hidden optimizations and how they affect real-world development.

Understanding Reactive Statement Optimization

Reactive statements in Svelte, marked with the `$:` syntax, are a core part of how reactivity works. What is less obvious is that Svelte treats them with extreme precision at compile time.

When you write something like this:

```
<script>
    let width = 200;
    let height = 100;
    $: area = width * height;
</script>

<p>The area is {area} square pixels.</p>
```

the Svelte compiler does more than just re-calculate `area` every time anything changes. It **builds a dependency graph** at compile time. It knows exactly that `area` depends only on `width` and `height`. If another variable elsewhere in your script changes — for example, a theme color or a username — Svelte will not touch the `area` value because those variables are not linked.

This means that reactive updates are scoped to the exact variables that matter. No unnecessary recalculations occur. No wasted DOM updates happen. This is fundamentally different from frameworks that use proxy-based reactivity or require dirty-checking cycles.

To see the real impact of this optimization, consider a more complex situation:

```
<script>
    let width = 200;
    let height = 100;
    let borderWidth = 5;

    $: area = (width - 2 * borderWidth) * (height
 - 2 * borderWidth);
</script>

<p>Content area: {area} square pixels</p>
```

Here, `area` depends on `width`, `height`, and `borderWidth`. At compile time, Svelte captures all three dependencies. If you only change `borderWidth`, Svelte knows exactly to re-run the area calculation and update the DOM. It doesn't re-run unrelated logic.

This targeted precision allows your applications to stay fast even when managing dozens or hundreds of reactive variables.

Reducing Runtime Overhead with Static Analysis

Static analysis means that Svelte inspects your code at build time to predict its behavior without needing to actually run it. This is one of the most powerful aspects of the Svelte compiler.

For example, when you write a component like this:

```
<script>
    let message = "Hello, Svelte!";
</script>

<h1>{message}</h1>
```

Svelte knows that `message` is a simple string and that it doesn't change unless you explicitly reassign it. The compiler generates code that updates the `<h1>`

13

only when `message` is reassigned. It does not install watchers, proxies, or other runtime tracking mechanisms.

As a result, simple bindings in Svelte produce zero runtime cost after initial rendering, unless a real change occurs. This optimization applies not only to text nodes but also to attributes, styles, and classes bound dynamically.

Now think about this in the context of large-scale applications: if you have hundreds of components, each with dynamic parts, removing runtime observers across the board can eliminate thousands of unnecessary computations on every state change.

This is why Svelte applications tend to feel "snappier" and "lighter" compared to those built with frameworks that rely on runtime tracking.

Improving Event Handling Efficiency

Another key area where the Svelte compiler optimizes is in how it handles event listeners.

Suppose you attach a simple click handler to a button:

```
<button on:click={() => alert('Clicked!')}>Click
Me</button>
```

At first glance, you might expect that Svelte would generate a fresh function for every instance of this component. That could be wasteful if you had hundreds of such buttons on the page.

Instead, the compiler notices when inline event handlers are **static** — meaning they do not depend on any reactive values — and can **hoist them out** so that the same function instance is shared across all component instances.

If the event handler depends on dynamic values inside your component, such as reactive variables, then it must be recreated per instance. However, if it doesn't, Svelte saves memory and processing time by reusing the same event function.

To maximize this optimization yourself, you can move event handlers into named functions inside your `<script>` block:

```
<script>
```

```
    function handleClick() {
        alert('Clicked!');
    }
</script>

<button on:click={handleClick}>Click Me</button>
```

By writing event handlers as named functions, you help the compiler recognize opportunities to hoist and optimize. This pattern becomes critical when scaling up to applications with many interactive elements.

Dead Code Elimination for Leaner Bundles

Dead code elimination refers to the process of removing parts of the code that will never be executed or that are unnecessary for the final application.

Svelte's compiler aggressively removes unused variables, functions, and even entire sections of logic if they are not referenced by the template or reactive graph.

For example:

```
<script>
    let unused = 42;
    let used = "This shows up!";
</script>

<p>{used}</p>
```

Here, unused is completely stripped from the compiled output. It doesn't make it into your JavaScript bundle. You don't pay for it in download size, parsing time, or execution cost.

At scale, this optimization has a direct impact on application performance, especially for mobile users where download size and load time are critical.

One important thing to understand is that Svelte can only eliminate dead code when it can **deterministically** prove at compile time that the code is unused. If your code uses dynamic imports, runtime evaluations (eval), or dynamic property access, it might prevent dead code elimination.

Being aware of this helps you structure your applications in a way that makes them more amenable to compiler optimizations — avoiding excessive dynamic behavior unless absolutely necessary.

A Practical Demonstration

Let's build a simple exercise to make these concepts concrete.

Create two components: one written in a way that enables Svelte's optimizations and one that prevents them.

Optimized Component (Good Practice)

```
<script>
    let name = "Svelte Developer";

    function greet() {
        alert(`Hello, ${name}!`);
    }
</script>

<button on:click={greet}>
    Greet
</button>
```

In this example:

greet is a named function, allowing hoisting.

name is clearly reactive and referenced directly in the template.

The compiler generates efficient, targeted update code.

Non-Optimized Component (Poor Practice)

```
<script>
    let user = { name: "Svelte Developer" };
</script>

<button on:click={() => alert(`Hello,
${user.name}!`)}>
    Greet
</button>
```

In this example:

The inline event handler must be recreated for every component instance because it closes over `user`.

The object structure (`user.name`) can complicate static analysis if later mutated dynamically.

More runtime overhead results because of reduced hoisting and optimization opportunities.

By comparing the compiled outputs of these two components, you would notice that the first one generates cleaner, smaller, and faster code.

Svelte's compiler does a tremendous amount of hidden work for you — work that pays off directly in performance, bundle size, and responsiveness. But the compiler can only optimize as well as your code allows it to.

When you structure your code in a way that is predictable, declarative, and assignment-driven, you unlock the full potential of Svelte's optimization strategies.

As your applications grow larger, understanding and supporting these hidden optimizations is not optional — it becomes essential to maintain quality, speed, and maintainability at scale.

Fine-Tuning Code for Compiler Efficiency

When you work with Svelte at an advanced level, it is no longer enough to simply make your application "work." True expertise means writing code that not only functions correctly but also helps the compiler generate the most efficient output possible. Fine-tuning your code for compiler efficiency is about developing small, thoughtful habits that together result in faster load times, smoother user interactions, and more maintainable systems.

In Svelte, reactivity is built around **assignments**. Any time you assign a new value to a variable, the compiler knows that it must update any parts of the template or reactive graph that depend on that variable.

This behavior means that, whenever you want to trigger a reactive update, **you must reassign the variable itself** — not just mutate the value it points to.

Let's take an example:

```
<script>
    let items = ['Apple', 'Banana'];
</script>

{#each items as item}
    <p>{item}</p>
{/each}
```

Suppose you want to add a new item. If you simply mutate the array:

```
items.push('Cherry');
```

Svelte will not detect any change, because the `items` variable was not reassigned. The array changed internally, but from the compiler's perspective, `items` still points to the same array in memory.

To trigger an update properly, you need to create a new array and assign it back:

```
items = [...items, 'Cherry'];
```

This small habit — favoring reassignment over mutation — is key to keeping your applications reliably reactive. It ensures the compiler can efficiently target exactly what needs updating without guessing or scanning for changes at runtime.

This principle also applies to objects:

```
<script>
    let profile = { name: "Alice", age: 30 };
</script>

<h1>{profile.name}</h1>
```

If you want to update the user's name, do not mutate directly:

```
profile.name = "Bob"; // No reactivity triggered
```

Instead, you should reassign:

```
profile = { ...profile, name: "Bob" };
```

By creating a fresh object and assigning it, you give the compiler the signal it needs to efficiently update the DOM.

Keeping Dependencies Explicit in Reactive Statements

When writing reactive statements using `$:`, it's important to make dependencies as **explicit** as possible. The clearer you are, the better the compiler can optimize updates.

Consider the following pattern:

```
<script>
     let a = 5;
     let b = 10;

     $: sum = a + b;
</script>

<p>Sum is {sum}</p>
```

Here, it is crystal clear to the compiler that `sum` depends on `a` and `b`. Any time either changes, the sum should be recalculated.

However, if you bury your dependencies inside function calls, dynamic property accesses, or deep object structures, you can obscure these relationships. For example:

```
<script>
     let values = { a: 5, b: 10 };

     $: sum = calculate(values);

     function calculate(obj) {
          return obj.a + obj.b;
     }
</script>
```

In this case, Svelte knows that `sum` depends on `values`, but it cannot track which properties inside `values` matter. If you later mutate `values.a` directly, Svelte will not trigger an update because no reassignment occurred.

To help the compiler optimize, you should prefer direct and transparent relationships in reactive code. The more explicit your dependencies, the more surgical Svelte's updates can be.

Structuring Templates for Clarity and Efficiency

In Svelte, the way you structure your markup influences how the compiler generates update code. Keeping your templates clean and separating logic from markup wherever possible improves both clarity and compiler efficiency.

Take an example where you need to display a status message based on a user's login state:

```
<h2>{loggedIn ? 'Welcome back!' : 'Please log in'}</h2>
```

Although Svelte can handle inline conditionals like this, you gain clarity and allow better static analysis if you move logic into a `<script>` block:

```
<script>
    let loggedIn = false;
    $: statusMessage = loggedIn ? 'Welcome back!'
: 'Please log in';
</script>

<h2>{statusMessage}</h2>
```

Here, the compiler treats `statusMessage` as a direct dependency. When `loggedIn` changes, it recalculates `statusMessage` and updates the `<h2>`. The DOM update logic becomes simpler and more predictable.

Small improvements like this make a real difference as templates grow larger and more complex.

Preferring Named Functions for Event Handlers

Another important way to fine-tune your code is how you write event handlers. Inline anonymous functions can look convenient, but they often force the compiler to regenerate new function instances unnecessarily.

Suppose you have:

```
<button on:click={() => count +=
1}>Increment</button>
```

Every time the component is created or updated, a fresh function is created in memory. This is not a huge issue in small applications, but in large-scale apps with thousands of interactive elements, it adds up.

You can easily optimize by defining the handler separately:

```
<script>
    let count = 0;

    function increment() {
        count += 1;
    }
</script>

<button on:click={increment}>Increment</button>
```

Now the same function can be reused, memory pressure is reduced, and the compiler can further optimize the event binding process.

In bigger projects, this small shift helps preserve both performance and maintainability.

It is easy to focus on small technical tricks, but the bigger picture is about consistency. Fine-tuning code for the compiler is not about premature optimization. It is about writing clear, predictable, assignment-driven code that the compiler can understand completely.

Every reassignment, every dependency, every structure you create is a way of communicating with the compiler. The simpler and more direct your communication, the more efficient the resulting application will be.

By adopting a consistent coding style that favors clarity, reassignment, explicit dependencies, clean templates, and hoistable functions, you help Svelte produce the best output possible — not just today, but as your application evolves and grows.

The Svelte compiler is an incredibly powerful tool, but it works best when you write code that is simple, predictable, and declarative. Fine-tuning your code for efficiency is not about complicated tricks. It is about understanding how the compiler sees your code, and writing it in a way that makes optimization natural and inevitable.

Chapter 2: Advanced Reactivity Patterns

When you start with Svelte, learning to use $: reactive statements and simple reassignments feels intuitive and effortless. But as your applications grow, and as components interact across layers of complexity, managing reactivity demands more discipline. Mastering advanced reactivity patterns is what separates casual Svelte users from developers who can confidently build scalable, production-grade systems.

Reactivity in Svelte is powerful because it is designed to be simple. Yet true simplicity at scale comes not from avoiding complexity, but from managing it cleanly. In this chapter, we will explore how reactive statements and declarations work in depth, how to control complex dependency relationships without creating spaghetti logic, and how to structure application state so that even the largest applications remain predictable and maintainable.

Deep Dive into Reactive Statements and Declarations

Reactivity in Svelte is one of the framework's defining strengths. Unlike other JavaScript libraries where you must explicitly manage when updates happen, Svelte's compiler automatically handles updates based on how you write your code. Central to this are **reactive statements** and **reactive declarations**.

To use reactivity well at an advanced level, you need more than a basic familiarity with $: syntax. You need a precise understanding of how the compiler interprets your code, how dependencies are tracked, how evaluation order is determined, and how small choices you make can significantly influence performance and maintainability.

How Reactive Statements Actually Work

When you write a reactive statement using $:, Svelte analyzes the code inside that statement at **build time** — not at runtime — to detect which variables it depends on. The compiler then ensures that whenever any of those variables change, the reactive statement re-executes automatically.

The simplest form looks like this:

```
<script>
    let count = 0;

    $: doubled = count * 2;
</script>

<p>Doubled: {doubled}</p>
```

In this example, the reactive assignment to `doubled` depends solely on `count`. Whenever `count` is reassigned — whether incremented, decremented, or entirely overwritten — Svelte automatically re-runs the statement to update `doubled`, and in turn, updates the `<p>` element's content.

The crucial point here is that the compiler establishes the dependency graph at build time. It does not guess at runtime. It does not perform expensive dependency checking later. It knows immediately, in advance, that `doubled` depends only on `count`.

Because of this, you should write reactive statements in a way that makes dependencies as **clear and direct** as possible. If you introduce dynamic or hidden dependencies, you make optimization much harder for the compiler.

Order of Evaluation in Reactive Statements

In Svelte, reactive statements are evaluated in the order they appear in the `<script>` block. However, dependency relationships can modify that order when necessary.

Consider the following code:

```
<script>
    let width = 100;
    let height = 200;

    $: area = width * height;
    $: displayArea = `${area} square pixels`;
</script>

<p>{displayArea}</p>
```

Here, `area` must be computed before `displayArea`, because `displayArea` depends on `area`. Even though `displayArea` appears **after** `area` in code

23

order, Svelte detects the dependency chain and automatically ensures that `area` is updated first before recalculating `displayArea`.

This behavior ensures correctness even when your code gets complex. However, for clarity and maintainability, it is a good habit to structure your reactive statements **top-to-bottom** based on logical dependency, matching the order in which they should be computed whenever possible.

This makes it easier for both human readers and the compiler to process the code predictably.

Reactive Statements Without Assignments

Not every reactive statement needs to assign a value. You can use `$:` to run arbitrary side effects whenever dependencies change.

For example:

```
<script>
    let count = 0;

    $: {
        console.log(`The count is now ${count}`);
    }
</script>

<button on:click={() => count +=
1}>Increment</button>
```

Here, the block inside `$:` does not produce a value; it performs an action. Every time `count` changes, Svelte re-executes the block, logging the new value.

This pattern is useful when you need to trigger effects — like logging, calling a function, or updating something outside the DOM — based on reactive state.

However, you should be cautious when using side-effect reactive blocks extensively. Overusing side effects can make your component harder to reason about and may introduce subtle bugs if side effects are not properly scoped.

As a best practice, keep reactive assignments and side-effect reactive blocks **separate** unless the effect is tightly coupled with the reactive variables.

Dependency Detection and Dynamic Behavior

Svelte's reactivity model depends on **static analysis**. This means that the compiler must be able to **see** which variables are used inside a reactive statement directly at build time.

Suppose you write:

```
<script>
    let field = 'name';
    let values = { name: 'Alice', age: 30 };

    $: selectedValue = values[field];
</script>

<p>{selectedValue}</p>
```

At first glance, this looks fine. But there is a subtle catch: Svelte can only tell that `selectedValue` depends on `values` and `field` — it cannot tell which specific property inside `values` matters. Because the property accessed depends dynamically on the value of `field`, the dependency graph becomes looser.

As a result, if you mutate `values.name` directly without reassigning `values` or changing `field`, the reactive statement won't know to re-run.

This limitation is why **mutations** without reassignment often fail to trigger updates in Svelte. To ensure correct reactivity, you must **reassign** the dependent variable itself, like so:

```
values = { ...values, name: 'Bob' };
```

or

```
field = 'age';
```

Both approaches signal to Svelte that something important changed, prompting a reevaluation of the dependent reactive statements.

This distinction — between direct, statically analyzable dependencies and dynamic, runtime dependencies — is critical to writing reliable reactive code in large applications.

Practical Example: Building a Reactive Calculator

To really understand how reactive statements and declarations work together, let's build a simple practical example: a calculator that updates automatically based on user input.

Here is a full working example:

```
<script>
    let num1 = 0;
    let num2 = 0;

    $: sum = num1 + num2;
    $: difference = num1 - num2;
    $: product = num1 * num2;
    $: quotient = num2 !== 0 ? num1 / num2 :
'Undefined';
</script>

<div>
    <input type="number" bind:value={num1}>
    <input type="number" bind:value={num2}>
</div>

<div>
    <p>Sum: {sum}</p>
    <p>Difference: {difference}</p>
    <p>Product: {product}</p>
    <p>Quotient: {quotient}</p>
</div>
```

In this example:

Every arithmetic result is declared using a simple reactive statement.

All dependencies are direct and static — no dynamic property accesses or hidden lookups.

No unnecessary recomputations occur; only the exact reactive statements that depend on the changed inputs are re-evaluated.

If you inspect the compiled output, you would see that the Svelte compiler generates minimal, direct JavaScript updates for each operation, with no wasteful diffing or re-rendering logic.

This is the **ideal** use of Svelte's reactivity system: explicit, predictable, tightly scoped, and fully optimized at build time.

Svelte's reactive statements and declarations are simple at the surface, but mastering them deeply transforms how you build applications. They offer a precise, powerful, and highly optimized model — but only if you respect the way the compiler reads and analyzes your code.

By making your dependencies clear, by structuring your reactivity logically, and by writing in a way that reveals relationships rather than hiding them, you unlock the full power of Svelte's compiled reactivity. As applications grow, these principles ensure that your interfaces remain fast, predictable, and maintainable — no matter how complex the underlying logic becomes.

Managing Complex Reactive Dependencies

When applications are small, reactivity in Svelte feels almost effortless. Variables change, updates happen, and everything stays easy to reason about. But as your projects grow larger, reactive relationships inevitably become more layered and interdependent. A change in one part of your data can cascade across multiple components and calculations if you are not careful.

Managing complex reactive dependencies well is what makes the difference between an application that feels snappy and reliable, and one that feels fragile, chaotic, and slow to maintain. To master advanced Svelte development, you need to understand not just how reactivity works, but how to control it precisely across large interconnected systems.

The Nature of Dependency Chains in Svelte

Every time you create a reactive statement or declaration, you are creating a dependency. That dependency connects variables together so that when one changes, others are updated automatically.

Simple chains are easy to manage. For example:

```
<script>
```

```
    let a = 2;
    let b = a * 3;
    let c = b + 5;

    $: sum = c + a;
</script>

<p>{sum}</p>
```

In this case, `sum` depends on both `c` and `a`, and `c` itself depends on `b`, which depends on `a`. Svelte's compiler builds this graph automatically at compile time, ensuring that changes propagate through the correct sequence of calculations.

However, problems start when dependency chains become too wide, too deep, or too entangled. If many unrelated parts of your application depend on the same variables — or worse, on side effects of computations involving those variables — you end up with a **reactive explosion**. One tiny change can cause a surprising amount of recalculation and DOM updates, hurting both performance and maintainability.

The key to managing complexity is **structuring dependencies intentionally**, limiting how far and how wide reactivity can spread.

Isolating Reactive Concerns with Intermediate Variables

One of the most effective strategies for managing complex reactivity is **introducing intermediate reactive variables** that localize dependencies.

Suppose you are building a profile editor with multiple sections: basic info, contact details, and security settings. You might be tempted to write something like this:

```
<script>
    let profile = {
        name: 'Alice',
        email: 'alice@example.com',
        password: 'secret'
    };
```

```
      $: isProfileValid = profile.name.length > 0 &&
profile.email.includes('@') &&
profile.password.length >= 6;
</script>

{#if isProfileValid}
      <p>Profile is valid.</p>
{:else}
      <p>Profile is incomplete or invalid.</p>
{/if}
```

At first, this looks clean. But as soon as you start adding more fields, more rules, or more complex validations, `isProfileValid` becomes a tangled knot of logic that depends on the entire `profile` object.

A better structure is to **break down concerns**:

```
<script>
      let name = 'Alice';
      let email = 'alice@example.com';
      let password = 'secret';

      $: isNameValid = name.length > 0;
      $: isEmailValid = email.includes('@');
      $: isPasswordValid = password.length >= 6;

      $: isProfileValid = isNameValid &&
isEmailValid && isPasswordValid;
</script>

{#if isProfileValid}
      <p>Profile is valid.</p>
{:else}
      <p>Profile is incomplete or invalid.</p>
{/if}
```

Now, each piece of validation is its own reactive unit. When the user edits their email, only `isEmailValid` re-computes — not the entire profile validity logic unnecessarily. This fine-grained reactivity reduces cognitive load, minimizes recomputation, and keeps performance predictable.

Breaking large dependency chains into smaller, isolated, focused reactive blocks is one of the most valuable habits you can develop when working with Svelte at scale.

Avoiding Unnecessary Global State Dependencies

Another common source of complexity is tying too much logic to global state unnecessarily. When components depend directly on global stores or top-level reactive variables, small changes can ripple through many unrelated parts of the application.

Suppose you have a global user store:

```
// stores/user.js
import { writable } from 'svelte/store';

export const user = writable({ name: 'Alice', role: 'admin' });
```

If your navigation component, your settings page, your footer, and even some modals all depend on $user, any change to the user object triggers updates across all those areas.

While sometimes necessary, this kind of widespread dependency should be handled carefully. Instead of every component reading directly from the store, it can be better to **derive only the specific pieces of data needed locally**.

For example:

```
<script>
    import { user } from '../stores/user.js';

    $: userName = $user.name;
</script>

<p>Hello, {userName}</p>
```

By creating a local reactive variable like userName, you limit the scope of reactivity to just what the component cares about. If the user object changes elsewhere — for example, if an admin toggles a different role — this component will only update if the name field was affected.

Isolating reactivity in this way prevents unnecessary re-renders and improves performance, especially in applications where state changes frequently.

Recognizing and Managing Indirect Dependencies

A more subtle challenge in managing complex reactivity is dealing with **indirect dependencies** — cases where variable A depends on variable B, but only through an intermediate calculation or function.

Consider this:

```
<script>
    let radius = 5;

    function calculateArea(r) {
        return Math.PI * r * r;
    }

    $: area = calculateArea(radius);
</script>

<p>Area: {area}</p>
```

In this case, `area` depends on `radius`, but the dependency is mediated through the `calculateArea` function.

This pattern is safe because `calculateArea` is **pure** — it has no side effects, and its output depends solely on its input. Svelte tracks the dependency on `radius` accurately.

But if you introduce functions that use external variables, you risk hiding important dependencies from the compiler.

Example of a risky structure:

```
<script>
    let width = 5;
    let height = 10;

    function calculateArea() {
        return width * height;
    }
}
```

```
    $: area = calculateArea();
</script>
```

Here, `calculateArea` does not receive parameters. It accesses `width` and `height` from the outer scope. While this still works, it obscures the dependencies slightly. It is cleaner and safer to pass dependencies as arguments explicitly:

```
<script>
    let width = 5;
    let height = 10;

    function calculateArea(w, h) {
        return w * h;
    }

    $: area = calculateArea(width, height);
</script>
```

This style keeps the dependency graph easy for both you and the compiler to reason about. You know at a glance which variables affect `area`, and Svelte's static analysis remains fully effective.

Whenever you use functions inside reactive declarations, favor passing dependencies explicitly. This strengthens the clarity of your reactivity and avoids hard-to-debug issues later when application complexity grows.

Practical Exercise: Refactoring a Reactive Chain

Let's walk through a small exercise where we refactor messy reactivity into clean, manageable pieces.

Suppose you start with this:

```
<script>
    let length = 5;
    let width = 10;
    let unit = 'cm';

    $: area = length * width;
    $: description = `The area is ${area}
${unit}²`;
```

```
</script>

<p>{description}</p>
```

At first glance, this seems fine. But what happens when you add a height field and start handling volume as well? The reactive web grows rapidly.

Refactor it like this:

```
<script>
    let length = 5;
    let width = 10;
    let height = 3;
    let unit = 'cm';

    $: area = length * width;
    $: volume = area * height;
    $: areaDescription = `${area} ${unit}²`;
    $: volumeDescription = `${volume} ${unit}³`;
</script>

<p>Area: {areaDescription}</p>
<p>Volume: {volumeDescription}</p>
```

Now, `area` and `volume` are separated logically. Descriptions are also computed separately. Each reactive variable has a clear and direct responsibility.

If the user changes only the height, only `volume` and `volumeDescription` are recomputed. `area` and `areaDescription` stay untouched.

This pattern of **layered, localized reactivity** scales beautifully into large projects without creating confusion or unnecessary recomputations.

Managing complex reactive dependencies in Svelte is a skill built through careful structuring, deliberate separation of concerns, and consistent writing practices.

By isolating reactive concerns, avoiding unnecessary entanglement with global state, favoring explicit dependency passing, and layering reactivity in clean chains, you build applications that remain fast, stable, and easy to understand — even as their size and complexity grow.

Structuring State for Large Applications

In the early stages of building an application, managing state inside individual components feels simple and manageable. You define a few local variables, create reactive statements where needed, and bind inputs directly to values. Everything stays neat because the surface area is small.

But as your application grows — when components start needing to communicate, when business logic spreads across features, and when different parts of your UI depend on shared pieces of information — the way you structure state becomes critical. Without deliberate design, state can quickly become fragmented, tangled, and difficult to maintain.

In large-scale Svelte applications, structuring state properly is not just about managing data flow. It's about building systems that remain predictable, modular, testable, and scalable, even as you add new features or multiple developers join the project.

Understanding the Limits of Local Component State

Local state — simple variables declared inside a component's `<script>` block — is perfectly fine when the state is used exclusively inside that component.

For instance, if you are building a simple modal that tracks whether it is open or closed, keeping `let isOpen = false;` inside the component makes sense.

But if multiple components need access to the same piece of state — for example, if a navbar, a sidebar, and a main page component all need to know whether a user is logged in — keeping that state local quickly breaks down. You would either have to pass props through multiple layers (known as "prop drilling") or duplicate logic across components, both of which lead to brittle, hard-to-maintain code.

Recognizing when local state needs to **evolve into shared, centralized state** is a key skill in building large applications.

Introducing Writable Stores for Shared State

In Svelte, **stores** provide a clean and efficient way to manage shared state across multiple components without creating unnecessary coupling.

A store is simply an object with a `.subscribe` method that allows components to react to changes over time. Writable stores, provided by Svelte's core API, allow both reading and updating values.

Suppose you are building an e-commerce site, and you need a shopping cart that multiple components can access and update. Here's how you would structure it:

First, create a dedicated store module:

```
// stores/cart.js
import { writable } from 'svelte/store';

export const cartItems = writable([]);
```

This creates a store that holds an array of cart items.

Now, inside any component, you can import the store and interact with it:

```
<script>
    import { cartItems } from '../stores/cart.js';

    function addItemToCart(item) {
        cartItems.update(items => [...items,
item]);
    }
</script>

<button on:click={() => addItemToCart({ id: 1,
name: 'Laptop' })}>
    Add to Cart
</button>
```

Because the store is reactive, any component using `$cartItems` will automatically update when the contents of the cart change.

This approach eliminates the need to manually pass props across unrelated parts of the application. It creates a **single source of truth** for cart data, making the application easier to reason about and debug.

In large applications, organizing your major shared state into carefully designed writable stores keeps complexity contained and reduces the number of unnecessary re-renders dramatically.

Using Derived Stores for Computed State

As applications become more complex, you will often need to compute values based on other state variables — totals, filtered lists, validation flags, and so on.

Instead of duplicating logic across components, you can use **derived stores** to create automatically updating computed values.

Continuing with the shopping cart example, you might want to calculate the total number of items or the total cost. You can define a derived store:

```js
// stores/cart.js
import { writable, derived } from 'svelte/store';

export const cartItems = writable([]);

export const cartTotal = derived(cartItems,
$cartItems =>
    $cartItems.reduce((total, item) => total +
item.price, 0)
);
```

Now, any component can subscribe to $cartTotal and get a real-time updated total price without manually recalculating it.

Derived stores allow you to express relationships between pieces of state declaratively. They make dependencies explicit and keep logic centralized and predictable, which is essential when managing hundreds of variables across a large system.

Separating Business State and UI State

In large applications, it is important to distinguish between **business state** and **UI state**.

Business state represents the actual data and domain logic of your application — things like users, orders, authentication tokens, inventory, and so on. These should be stored centrally in writable or derived stores, shared across components as needed.

UI state represents temporary interface concerns — whether a modal is open, which tab is active, whether a form is expanded. These are often best kept local to the component they affect.

Mixing these two kinds of state leads to confusing reactivity patterns. For example, if you tie whether a modal is open to a global authentication store, you create unnecessary coupling between independent parts of your app.

A clean separation helps with scaling. Business state flows through your application in a predictable, manageable way. UI state stays lightweight, isolated, and easier to modify without unintended side effects.

Scoping State with Context API

Sometimes, you need to share state across deeply nested components without making everything global.

Svelte's **Context API** allows you to provide values at a parent component level and access them in any deeply nested child, without prop drilling.

For example, you might have a `DashboardLayout` component that needs to pass user preferences like theme and language settings to many child components.

You can set context in the parent:

```
<script context="module">
    import { setContext } from 'svelte';

    const preferences = {
        theme: 'dark',
        language: 'en'
    };

    setContext('preferences', preferences);
</script>

<slot />
```

Then access it in any descendant component:

```
<script>
    import { getContext } from 'svelte';
```

```
      const preferences = getContext('preferences');
</script>

<p>Current theme: {preferences.theme}</p>
```

Using context properly allows you to scope shared state to specific areas of your app rather than making everything globally available, which keeps your architecture cleaner and more modular as you scale.

Real-World Example: Structuring State in a Project Management App

Suppose you are building a project management tool with users, projects, tasks, and notifications.

A clean state structure might look like this:

User Store: holds current user information and authentication status.

Projects Store: holds a list of projects the user has access to.

Tasks Store: holds tasks related to currently active projects.

Notifications Store: manages real-time user notifications.

Each piece is separated into its own store module. Each store manages only its own concern. Components subscribe only to the stores they care about, rather than to a massive monolithic global state object.

In addition, UI state — like whether the sidebar is collapsed or which modal is open — stays local to components like `Sidebar.svelte` and `Modal.svelte`, rather than leaking into global business stores.

This separation allows you to add new features — like tagging tasks or favoriting projects — without disrupting unrelated parts of the application. It keeps growth manageable and technical debt under control.

Structuring state for large applications in Svelte is not about adding complexity. It's about introducing the right amount of structure at the right time, keeping shared business logic centralized, keeping UI concerns local, and making reactive relationships clear and predictable.

38

Chapter 3: Stores and Contexts at Scale

When applications stay small, managing local state inside components or passing a few props here and there feels natural and efficient. But as projects grow — when multiple components need to react to the same source of truth, when updates come from different areas of the application, and when state needs to be shared cleanly across unrelated parts of the interface — local strategies start to strain under the weight.

At scale, you need better tools and architectural patterns. In Svelte, those tools are **stores** and the **Context API**. Together, they allow you to move from local, ad-hoc state management to centralized, modular, scalable state systems that remain predictable even as complexity rises.

In this chapter, we will work through the advanced use of writable, readable, and derived stores. We will create fully custom stores when the standard primitives aren't enough. We will see how to use Context API responsibly to share state without unnecessary global coupling. And we will learn how to build store systems that support real-world scalability across full applications.

Custom Stores: Writable, Readable, Derived, and Custom APIs

When building real-world Svelte applications, managing reactive state across multiple components and modules becomes a critical concern. At a small scale, local component state using plain variables can be enough. But as the number of components grows, and when multiple parts of the application need to react to the same piece of information, local state management quickly reaches its limit.

Svelte's store system provides a clean, flexible way to manage shared, reactive state. But using stores effectively — especially creating custom, scalable store architectures — requires a deeper understanding than just using $storeName inside a template.

Writable Stores: The Foundation of Shared State

A writable store is the most fundamental type of store in Svelte. It holds a single piece of reactive state and provides methods to **read**, **write**, and **update** that value.

To create a writable store, you import `writable` from `svelte/store` and initialize it with a starting value:

```
import { writable } from 'svelte/store';

export const counter = writable(0);
```

Here, `counter` is a store holding the numeric value `0`. It exposes three methods:

`subscribe` — allows components to reactively use the store

`set` — allows you to replace the value

`update` — allows you to change the value based on its current state

Using the store inside a Svelte component looks like this:

```
<script>
    import { counter } from
'../stores/counter.js';
</script>

<button on:click={() => $counter += 1}>
    Clicked {$counter} times
</button>
```

The `$counter` syntax automatically subscribes to the store and re-renders the component whenever the value changes. When you modify `$counter`, Svelte automatically calls `set` behind the scenes.

If you prefer, you can use the `update` method explicitly:

```
counter.update(n => n + 1);
```

This approach is particularly useful when the new value depends on the previous one, because it ensures consistency even if multiple updates happen in a short period of time.

Writable stores form the backbone of many real-world Svelte projects. Any piece of global or shared state — like authentication information, UI settings, or form data — often starts life as a simple writable store.

Readable Stores: Controlled Data Streams

Sometimes you need a store where the data is reactive but **external code should not be allowed to modify it directly**. For example, a clock that ticks every second, or a remote API feed updating asynchronously.

This is where readable stores are essential.

A readable store still allows subscription, but only the internal logic inside the store can update its value.

Here's an example of a readable store providing the current time:

```
import { readable } from 'svelte/store';

export const currentTime = readable(new Date(),
function start(set) {
    const interval = setInterval(() => {
        set(new Date());
    }, 1000);

    return function stop() {
        clearInterval(interval);
    };
});
```

In this case:

currentTime starts with the current date and time.

Every second, it updates by calling set(new Date()).

When no components are subscribed anymore, the stop function is called to clean up the interval.

Components use it the same way:

```
<script>
    import { currentTime } from
'../stores/currentTime.js';
```

```
</script>

<p>Current Time:
{$currentTime.toLocaleTimeString()}</p>
```

This structure is perfect for read-only reactive data streams. It protects against accidental external modification and keeps your data flow controlled.

Derived Stores: Automatic Computed Values

Often, you need to create **computed** state — values that are based on other reactive values but should update automatically whenever dependencies change.

Svelte's `derived` function makes this easy.

Suppose you have a cart store containing an array of items, and you want to compute the total price.

Start with your writable store:

```
import { writable } from 'svelte/store';

export const cart = writable([
    { name: 'Laptop', price: 1200 },
    { name: 'Headphones', price: 200 }
]);
```

Now, create a derived store based on `cart`:

```
import { derived } from 'svelte/store';
import { cart } from './cart.js';

export const cartTotal = derived(cart, $cart =>
    $cart.reduce((sum, item) => sum + item.price,
0)
);
```

Every time the `cart` store updates, the `cartTotal` automatically recalculates without you needing to manually trigger anything.

In your component:

```
<script>
```

```
        import { cartTotal } from '../stores/cart.js';
</script>

<p>Total: ${$cartTotal}</p>
```

Derived stores are the key to **keeping computation and display logic separate**. You avoid cluttering components with logic about how values are computed. Instead, you centralize and encapsulate that logic inside stores.

This separation makes larger applications much easier to maintain because when the rules for calculation change, you only update the store, not every component that uses the data.

Creating Fully Custom Stores with Additional APIs

Writable, readable, and derived stores are powerful on their own. But sometimes, you need stores that offer specialized behavior — custom actions that modify internal state in specific ways.

In these cases, you can build your own custom stores by wrapping a writable internally and exposing your own API.

Here's an example: a todo store with built-in add, toggle, and clear functions.

```
import { writable } from 'svelte/store';

function createTodoStore() {
    const { subscribe, set, update } =
writable([]);

    return {
        subscribe,
        add: (text) => update(todos => [...todos,
{ text, done: false }]),
        toggle: (index) => update(todos => {
            const updated = [...todos];
            updated[index].done =
!updated[index].done;
            return updated;
        }),
        clear: () => set([])
```

```
        };
}

export const todos = createTodoStore();
```

Notice a few important points here:

The internal writable manages the actual data.

`subscribe` is exposed unchanged, so components can still use `$todos`.

Custom methods (`add`, `toggle`, `clear`) provide **controlled mutation** paths for the state.

No external component can modify the state directly except through the intended API.

Using this custom store in a component:

```
<script>
    import { todos } from '../stores/todos.js';

    let newTodo = '';
</script>

<input bind:value={newTodo} placeholder="New todo">
<button on:click={() => {
    todos.add(newTodo);
    newTodo = '';
}}>Add</button>

<ul>
    {#each $todos as todo, index}
        <li>
            <input type="checkbox"
checked={todo.done} on:change={() =>
todos.toggle(index)}>
            {todo.text}
        </li>
    {/each}
</ul>

<button on:click={todos.clear}>Clear All</button>
```

This custom store structure gives you the best of both worlds:

Reactivity remains fully automatic and ergonomic.

State transitions are centralized, making them easy to test, validate, and maintain.

Components stay focused only on **what** needs to happen, not **how** it happens internally.

In real-world applications — like user authentication, shopping carts, messaging systems, or notification managers — custom stores become essential for organizing complex behavior without creating tangled, hard-to-maintain code.

Writable, readable, and derived stores give you everything you need to manage reactive shared state across components, pages, and modules. But real mastery comes when you start designing **custom store APIs** — specialized, intentional interfaces that manage their own complexity internally while keeping the components that use them clean and focused.

By structuring your stores thoughtfully and wrapping them in clean APIs, you unlock the ability to build large, reactive systems in Svelte that stay fast, maintainable, and easy to reason about — no matter how many features or moving parts your application adds over time.

Sharing State with Context API

When working on large applications, you often face situations where passing data through props becomes tedious and messy. Having to thread values down through multiple layers of components — a practice called **prop drilling** — quickly leads to bloated, tangled code that is hard to maintain.

Svelte offers a clean and powerful solution to this problem: the **Context API**. It allows you to set a value in a parent component and retrieve it in any descendant component, no matter how deeply nested, without manually passing it through intermediate components.

When used correctly, Context helps you structure your applications more cleanly, keeps component interfaces simple, and promotes better separation of concerns.

At its core, the Context API has two fundamental operations: **setContext** and **getContext**.

`setContext(key, value)` — This is called in a parent component to provide a value associated with a specific key.

`getContext(key)` — This is called in a child component to retrieve the value associated with that key.

Both the key and value can be anything, but the key must uniquely identify the context. Typically, developers use strings, symbols, or imported constants as keys to avoid accidental collisions.

Context only applies **down the component hierarchy**. Children and their descendants can access values set by their ancestors. But siblings and parents do not have access to each other's contexts unless specifically designed.

This scoping behavior is deliberate. It ensures that Context remains a structured, predictable way of sharing data without accidentally leaking across unrelated parts of the application.

Basic Example: Theme Management

Suppose you are building an application that supports light and dark themes. You want to allow all deeply nested components to know the current theme without passing it explicitly through props.

You can set up a context at a high level in your application, such as in a layout or a page component.

First, setting the context:

```svelte
<!-- ThemeProvider.svelte -->
<script>
    import { setContext } from 'svelte';

    const theme = 'dark';
    setContext('theme', theme);
</script>

<slot />
```

Here, the `ThemeProvider` component sets a context value with the key `'theme'`. It provides the string `'dark'` as the value.

Any component rendered inside this provider can now access the theme without having to receive it through props.

Retrieving the context in a child:

```
<!-- Header.svelte -->
<script>
    import { getContext } from 'svelte';

    const theme = getContext('theme');
</script>

<h1 class={theme}>Welcome!</h1>
```

When `Header.svelte` runs `getContext('theme')`, it retrieves the value `'dark'` provided by its ancestor.

Now, the `Header` component can style itself based on the current theme without the parent having to pass the theme explicitly.

This keeps the component interface clean. `Header.svelte` does not need to know who provides the theme. It simply trusts that it is available if needed.

Using Stores Inside Context

The Context API becomes even more powerful when you combine it with **stores**. Instead of setting simple static values like strings, you can set stores as context values, allowing child components to reactively subscribe to shared data.

Suppose your theme is not static but needs to change dynamically at runtime. You can build a theme store:

```
// stores/theme.js
import { writable } from 'svelte/store';

export const theme = writable('light');
```

Then, set the store into context:

```
<!-- ThemeProvider.svelte -->
<script>
    import { setContext } from 'svelte';
    import { theme } from '../stores/theme.js';

    setContext('theme', theme);
</script>

<slot />
```

In a child component:

```
<!-- Header.svelte -->
<script>
    import { getContext } from 'svelte';

    const themeStore = getContext('theme');
</script>

<h1 class={$themeStore}>Welcome!</h1>
```

Here, `$themeStore` gives the current theme reactively. If the theme changes from `'light'` to `'dark'`, the `Header` component automatically updates without needing to receive any new props.

This pattern is powerful for building large applications where different parts of the UI need to react to shared, dynamic state without being tightly coupled together.

Scoped vs Global: When to Use Context Instead of Stores

Context and stores solve different problems. Understanding when to use each properly is key to maintaining clean application architecture.

Use stores when state is truly global and needs to be accessed across unrelated parts of the application, like authentication status, notifications, or user profiles.

Use Context when state is scoped to a specific part of the component tree and should not leak globally, like theme settings inside a specific layout, form validation context inside a form component, or wizard state inside a multi-step component.

For example, if you are building an admin dashboard where different users might have different active configurations or permissions while inside their session, scoping this per dashboard instance using Context makes sense. You avoid polluting the global state with user-specific, session-specific details that do not concern other parts of the app.

Context gives you the flexibility to build **self-contained component systems** that provide and consume state internally without exposing unnecessary complexity to the rest of the application.

Practical Real-World Example: Multi-Step Form

Suppose you are building a multi-step form where several components need access to the shared form data, the current step, and navigation functions like `nextStep` and `prevStep`.

You can encapsulate everything using a store and Context together.

First, define the form state:

```
// stores/formState.js
import { writable } from 'svelte/store';

export const formData = writable({
    name: '',
    email: '',
    age: ''
});

export const currentStep = writable(1);
```

Now, create a provider component:

```
<!-- FormProvider.svelte -->
<script>
    import { setContext } from 'svelte';
    import { formData, currentStep } from
'../stores/formState.js';

    function nextStep() {
        currentStep.update(n => n + 1);
    }
```

```
    function prevStep() {
        currentStep.update(n => Math.max(1, n -
1));
    }

    setContext('form', {
        formData,
        currentStep,
        nextStep,
        prevStep
    });
</script>

<slot />
```

Then, in a child component that handles one step of the form:

```
<!-- StepOne.svelte -->
<script>
    import { getContext } from 'svelte';

    const { formData, nextStep } =
getContext('form');

    let name = '';

    function handleNext() {
        formData.update(data => ({ ...data, name
}));
        nextStep();
    }
</script>

<input bind:value={name} placeholder="Your name">
<button on:click={handleNext}>Next</button>
```

Each step component can independently access and update shared form state without worrying about prop chains or global store pollution. The form state remains scoped neatly to the form flow, controlled cleanly through Context.

This approach keeps large, multi-component workflows clean, modular, and easy to expand or refactor later.

The Context API is a precision tool. When used thoughtfully, it allows you to share state cleanly inside specific parts of your component hierarchy without creating tight coupling or leaking complexity globally.

By combining Context with stores and encapsulating functionality in provider components, you build scalable Svelte systems where components stay small, focused, and predictable — exactly the qualities you need as your applications grow in size and complexity.

Building Modular, Scalable Store Systems

In smaller projects, it's tempting to gather all shared state into a handful of writable stores and call it a day. You might have a `user` store here, a `cart` store there, and a few random configuration stores scattered throughout your application. It works at first because the surface area is small and easy to reason about.

But as your application grows — when teams expand, when features multiply, and when responsibilities start overlapping — unstructured store systems quickly become a source of confusion and technical debt. Changes to one part of the state can have unexpected side effects elsewhere. Store files become bloated. Maintenance becomes painful.

At scale, **modularity and clear organization** in your store systems is not just a matter of style. It is a necessity for long-term project health.

Building modular, scalable store systems in Svelte is about giving each concern its proper place, ensuring clean separation of responsibilities, and making state management predictable and maintainable across a growing application.

Defining Clear State Domains

The first principle of modular store design is to recognize that **not all state is the same**. Different kinds of data serve different purposes, belong to different parts of the system, and change under different conditions.

In a real-world e-commerce application, for example, you might deal with:

User authentication status and profile information

Shopping cart contents

Product listings and filters

UI preferences like theme and language

Notifications for the user

Instead of lumping all of this into a giant `globalStore.js` file, it is much cleaner to separate it into logical domains.

A clean directory structure for your stores might look like this:

src/

  stores/

    auth.js

    cart.js

    products.js

    ui.js

    notifications.js

Each file is responsible for managing only one type of state. This way, when you need to make changes to how cart management works, you don't risk accidentally interfering with authentication or UI settings.

This modular structure reflects the natural mental model of the application and helps future developers (or your future self) immediately find what they need to modify or debug.

Creating Dedicated Store Modules

Inside each store module, you should encapsulate **not just the store variable itself**, but also any logic needed to manipulate that part of the state.

Let's build a proper cart store as a full example:

```
// stores/cart.js
import { writable, derived } from 'svelte/store';

function createCart() {
```

```
        const { subscribe, update, set } =
writable([]);

    return {
        subscribe,
        addItem: (item) => update(items =>
[...items, item]),
        removeItem: (id) => update(items =>
items.filter(item => item.id !== id)),
        clearCart: () => set([]),
        totalPrice: derived(writable([]), $items
=> $items.reduce((total, item) => total +
item.price, 0))
    };
}

export const cart = createCart();
```

Notice that the store module does a few important things:

It wraps the basic writable functionality inside a custom API (addItem, removeItem, clearCart).

It keeps all logic for modifying the cart inside the module itself.

It prepares a derived computation (totalPrice) closely tied to the cart's behavior.

Components that use the cart do not need to know how items are managed internally. They simply call cart.addItem(item) or subscribe to $cart.totalPrice.

This separation protects your system from accidental misuse and centralizes responsibility for each domain's logic.

If later you need to add features like persisting the cart to localStorage, you can modify createCart() without changing dozens of unrelated components.

Managing Cross-Store Dependencies

Sometimes, pieces of state need to interact. For example, you might want the list of products available to a user to depend on their authentication status or their selected filters.

Instead of manually wiring together subscriptions inside components, **derived stores** provide a clean, scalable solution.

Suppose you have a products store:

```js
// stores/products.js
import { writable, derived } from 'svelte/store';
import { user } from './auth.js';

export const products = writable([]);

export const availableProducts = derived(
    [products, user],
    ([$products, $user]) => {
        if (!$user) return [];
        return $products.filter(product =>
product.region === $user.region);
    }
);
```

Here:

products contains all products from the database.

availableProducts automatically derives a filtered list based on the current logged-in user's region.

Components subscribe to $availableProducts without worrying about how user information affects product availability. The logic is centralized, reusable, and easy to reason about.

Managing cross-store dependencies using derived stores keeps your components simple and your reactivity clean.

Namespacing and Scalability

In very large applications, especially ones that grow into hundreds of features or modules, it's useful to **namespace** your store APIs to prevent naming conflicts and improve clarity.

Suppose your application manages users, and you have both authentication and user settings to deal with. Instead of having ambiguous stores like `settings`, you could organize them properly:

```
// stores/auth.js
export const user = writable(null);
export const token = writable(null);

// stores/userSettings.js
export const preferences = writable({
    theme: 'light',
    language: 'en'
});
export const notificationsEnabled = writable(true);
```

In components, import stores by domain:

```
<script>
    import { user } from '../stores/auth.js';
    import { preferences } from
'../stores/userSettings.js';
</script>

<p>Logged in as: {$user?.name}</p>
<p>Preferred language: {$preferences.language}</p>
```

Keeping store concerns separated and properly named avoids confusion when your application eventually has dozens or hundreds of reactive pieces to track.

This structure also prepares you to move stores into **feature packages** later if needed, improving modularity even further.

Real-World Example: Organizing a SaaS Dashboard

Let's say you are building a SaaS dashboard with features like analytics, billing, team management, and notifications.

A proper modular store structure might look like:

src/

  stores/

    auth.js   **// User login state, tokens, permissions**

```
billing.js        // Subscription plans, invoices

analytics.js      // Metrics and charts

teams.js          // List of team members, roles

notifications.js// User alerts and system messages

ui.js             // Sidebar toggle, active page, modal open
states
```

Each module defines only the state and behavior relevant to its area.

If you hire new developers to join the project, they can immediately understand where to go when working on billing versus working on analytics.

If you expand into more SaaS products, you can version or package feature-specific stores independently.

If you want to lazy-load heavy features (e.g., load `analytics.js` only when the user opens the analytics page), this modularity makes it feasible.

This discipline pays off heavily in the later stages of a project when complexity naturally increases.

Building modular, scalable store systems in Svelte is about much more than just splitting files. It's about **thinking in clean domains**, **centralizing behavior**, **managing dependencies explicitly**, and **keeping your data flow predictable and maintainable**.

When you treat each feature or concern of your application as a cleanly separated store module, and when you connect stores carefully using derived logic where necessary, your project remains easy to understand, easy to extend, and resilient under growth.

Chapter 4: Dynamic Component Architecture

When you first start building applications in Svelte, the simplicity of defining components and composing them together feels effortless. Small applications flourish naturally. But as your project grows, the need for **dynamic**, **flexible**, and **highly reusable** component architectures becomes critical.

Dynamic architecture is not just about creating more components. It's about making components smarter — designing them to handle varying data, structures, and workflows without breaking, without duplication, and without being tightly coupled to specific use cases.

In this chapter, we'll work through how to structure components dynamically in Svelte using **advanced slot techniques**, **dynamic imports and lazy loading**, and **dependency injection patterns**. These practices form the backbone of scalable, maintainable front-end systems.

Advanced Slot Usage and Reusable Components

When you first begin working with Svelte, using slots feels like a simple way to inject child content into components. At a small scale, inserting plain text or elements through a basic `<slot />` works perfectly. But as your applications grow, your components need to handle more flexible layouts, dynamic structures, and complex data passing.

Mastering **advanced slot usage** is one of the most important skills you can develop for building truly **reusable**, **scalable**, and **dynamic** Svelte components. Instead of rewriting slightly different versions of the same component for different pages or states, you build flexible components that adapt naturally to varying needs — all while keeping your code clean, concise, and powerful.

How Basic Slots Work

At the most basic level, a slot provides a placeholder inside a component where parent content will be injected.

Example:

```
<!-- Box.svelte -->
<div class="box">
    <slot />
</div>
```

Using it in a parent component:

```
<!-- App.svelte -->
<Box>
    <p>This is inside the box!</p>
</Box>
```

Here, the paragraph `<p>This is inside the box!</p>` is injected exactly where `<slot />` appears inside the `Box` component.

This basic usage is a foundation, but it only scratches the surface of what slots can do.

Using Named Slots for Structured Content

Real-world components often need **multiple insertion points**. For example, a modal might need separate areas for a header, a body, and a footer.

Svelte supports this by letting you **name slots**.

Here's how you define named slots:

```
<!-- Modal.svelte -->
<div class="modal">
    <header>
        <slot name="header" />
    </header>
    <section>
        <slot name="body" />
    </section>
    <footer>
        <slot name="footer" />
    </footer>
</div>
```

And here's how you use them:

```
<Modal>
    <h1 slot="header">Modal Title</h1>
    <p slot="body">This is the main content of the
modal.</p>
    <button slot="footer">Close</button>
</Modal>
```

Each piece of content is placed into the matching slot inside `Modal.svelte`. This makes your component much more flexible — it can be reused across different contexts with different structures, without needing to rewrite the internal markup.

Named slots are crucial when building components like:

Modals

Dialog boxes

Cards

Layouts with multiple regions (like header/sidebar/footer)

They allow your component to **define structure** while letting parent components **supply flexible content**.

Providing Fallback Content

Sometimes you want a slot to have default content when no content is supplied by the parent. This is called **fallback content**.

Here's an example:

```
<!-- Button.svelte -->
<button>
    <slot>Click me</slot>
</button>
```

If you use this button without providing any content:

<Button />

It will render "Click me" automatically.

If you do provide custom content:

```
<Button>Submit Form</Button>
```

then "Submit Form" will replace the fallback text.

Fallback content makes your components more resilient. It ensures that they always have something meaningful to display, even if the parent forgets to provide content.

In practice, you should always think about reasonable fallback defaults when building reusable components. Good defaults improve user experience and make your component APIs easier to use correctly.

Passing Data from Components with Slot Props

Sometimes it's not enough to just render parent content in a slot. You need to **pass data from the child component to the slot,** allowing the parent to customize rendering based on internal values.

This is where **slot props** come in.

Let's work through a practical example: a reusable list component.

```
<!-- ItemList.svelte -->
<script>
    export let items = [];
</script>

<ul>
    {#each items as item}
        <li>
            <slot {item} />
        </li>
    {/each}
</ul>
```

Here, item is passed into the slot for each list item.

Now, in the parent component:

```
<ItemList {items}>
    {#let item}
        <strong>{item.name}</strong> —
${item.price}
    {/let}
```

```
</ItemList>
```

Each `item` becomes available inside the `{#let}` block, and you can decide exactly how to render it.

Slot props are powerful for:

Custom-rendering data-driven UI components like tables, grids, menus

Providing fine-grained control over how child elements are displayed

Allowing maximum flexibility without bloating child components with assumptions

By exposing relevant data via slots, your components become **highly reusable** without losing power or expressiveness.

Practical Exercise: Building a Reusable Card Component with Slots

Let's build a full example that combines everything we've learned: fallback slots, named slots, and slot props.

First, the reusable component:

```
<!-- Card.svelte -->
<script>
    export let metadata = {};
</script>

<div class="card">
    <header class="card-header">
        <slot name="header">
            <h2>Default Title</h2>
        </slot>
    </header>

    <section class="card-body">
        <slot {metadata} />
    </section>

    <footer class="card-footer">
        <slot name="footer">
```

```
                    <small>Default Footer</small>
            </slot>
        </footer>
</div>
```

This `Card` component:

Defines three sections: header, body, and footer.

Provides default content for the header and footer if none is passed.

Passes the `metadata` object as a slot prop into the body slot.

Now, using the `Card`:

```
<Card {metadata}>
      <h1 slot="header">{metadata.title}</h1>

      {#let metadata}
           <p>{metadata.description}</p>
      {/let}

      <p slot="footer">Created on
{metadata.createdDate}</p>
</Card>
```

The parent:

Customizes the header and footer.

Accesses and displays the metadata inside the body dynamically.

This pattern creates a **truly reusable** and **dynamic** component:

It works with minimal setup if defaults are enough.

It becomes fully customizable when more control is needed.

It stays simple and clean inside both the reusable component and the consuming parent.

Advanced slot usage transforms your components from rigid templates into flexible, dynamic building blocks. By using named slots, fallback content, and slot props thoughtfully, you design components that can adapt to many different use cases without duplication, unnecessary complexity, or brittle assumptions.

The more carefully you structure your slots, the more power you give to the parent components — allowing maximum customization while keeping reusable components simple, focused, and stable.

Dynamic Imports, Lazy Loading, and Conditional Components

In the early stages of development, it's easy to build applications by simply importing and rendering components directly. At small scale, this works fine because there are only a handful of components, and the entire application can afford to load everything upfront without noticeable performance problems.

However, as real-world applications grow — with more pages, more components, more features — loading everything at once becomes a serious bottleneck. Your initial JavaScript bundle becomes heavy, page load times increase, and the user ends up waiting for parts of the app they might not even use during their session.

Dynamic imports and **lazy loading** offer a solution. They allow you to load components or modules only when they are needed, rather than bundling everything into the initial payload. Combined with **conditional rendering**, this strategy gives you fine-grained control over when and how parts of your application appear, based on user actions or application state.

Understanding Dynamic Imports in Svelte

In JavaScript, a **dynamic import** means importing a module at runtime instead of statically at build time. Svelte supports this natively, allowing you to load components only when they are actually needed.

Here's a basic example:

```
<script>
    let ModalComponent;
    let showModal = false;

    async function openModal() {
```

```
         const module = await
import('./Modal.svelte');
         ModalComponent = module.default;
         showModal = true;
     }
</script>

<button on:click={openModal}>
     Open Modal
</button>

{#if showModal && ModalComponent}
     <svelte:component this={ModalComponent} />
{/if}
```

In this setup:

The `ModalComponent` variable starts undefined.

When the user clicks the button, the `openModal()` function dynamically imports the `Modal.svelte` file.

Once the module loads, `ModalComponent` is set, and Svelte renders it using `<svelte:component>`.

This approach ensures that the code for the modal is **not included** in the main bundle. It's fetched **only when necessary**, improving initial page load performance.

Practical Real-World Example: Lazy Loading a Heavy Analytics Dashboard

Suppose your application includes an analytics dashboard filled with charts, tables, and data visualizations. Loading all that code upfront would hurt performance, especially for users who never even open the analytics section.

You can defer loading the dashboard until it's needed:

```
<script>
     let Dashboard;
     let isLoading = false;
     let showDashboard = false;
```

```
        async function loadDashboard() {
              isLoading = true;
              const module = await
import('./Dashboard.svelte');
              Dashboard = module.default;
              showDashboard = true;
              isLoading = false;
        }
</script>

<button on:click={loadDashboard}>
      View Analytics
</button>

{#if isLoading}
      <p>Loading dashboard...</p>
{/if}

{#if showDashboard && Dashboard}
      <svelte:component this={Dashboard} />
{/if}
```

Here, the dashboard:

Is not included in the initial JavaScript bundle.

Loads only after the user explicitly requests it.

Displays a loading state while the component is being fetched.

This technique keeps the core of your application lightweight and improves user experience by prioritizing essential content.

Using `<svelte:component>` for Conditional Components

Svelte provides a built-in `<svelte:component>` element that allows you to render different components dynamically at runtime based on a variable.

You can use it to conditionally load different UI elements without manually writing multiple {#if} blocks.

Example:

```
<script>
```

65

```
    import TextInput from './TextInput.svelte';
    import SelectInput from
'./SelectInput.svelte';

    let inputType = 'text';

    const componentMap = {
        text: TextInput,
        select: SelectInput
    };
</script>

<svelte:component this={componentMap[inputType]} />
```

Here:

inputType controls which component to render.

componentMap associates types with specific components.

<svelte:component> uses the appropriate component based on the current value.

This structure is extremely useful for:

Form builders

Dashboards with dynamic widgets

Layouts that change based on user settings or device type

Applications where the type of data being rendered varies dynamically

By combining dynamic imports with conditional components, you can even lazy-load different UI sections based on context, keeping your application responsive and efficient at every stage.

Handling Dynamic Imports More Elegantly with Wrappers

As your application grows, you may find yourself repeating the same dynamic import logic across many components. To clean this up, you can abstract dynamic loading into a reusable wrapper component.

Here's a simple LazyLoader.svelte:

```
<script>
    export let loader;
    let Component;
    let loading = true;

    onMount(async () => {
        const module = await loader();
        Component = module.default;
        loading = false;
    });
</script>

{#if loading}
    <p>Loading...</p>
{:else if Component}
    <svelte:component this={Component} />
{/if}
```

You can use this wrapper like so:

```
<LazyLoader loader={() =>
import('./HeavyComponent.svelte')} />
```

This approach:

Encapsulates the dynamic import logic.

Standardizes loading states.

Reduces repeated code.

Keeps your component files clean and focused.

In larger codebases, moving repetitive patterns like dynamic imports into reusable wrappers is a small but highly effective way to keep your architecture healthy.

Best Practices for Dynamic Components and Lazy Loading

While dynamic imports and conditional rendering are powerful, using them carelessly can introduce complexity or even degrade user experience. Here are important best practices to guide you:

Load only what you truly need. Don't over-fragment your codebase by splitting trivial components into separate chunks. Balance performance with maintainability.

Show loading indicators. Always give users visual feedback when components are loading. Even a simple spinner improves perceived responsiveness.

Handle errors gracefully. If a dynamic import fails (due to a network issue, for example), show a clear error message or offer a retry option.

Prefetch when appropriate. For features users are likely to use soon (e.g., when hovering over a link), you can preload components in the background using `import()` proactively.

Keep dynamic logic predictable. Use clear mapping structures (`componentMap`) and avoid complex conditional chains that are hard to debug.

Following these practices ensures that dynamic imports and lazy-loaded components **enhance** your application's performance without introducing unnecessary fragility.

Dynamic imports, lazy loading, and conditional components give you powerful ways to optimize both the **performance** and **architecture** of your Svelte applications. By loading only what is needed, when it is needed, you create experiences that are faster, more responsive, and more scalable — all without sacrificing flexibility or developer productivity.

Mastering these techniques is essential when building professional-grade, production-ready applications that serve real users at real scale.

Dependency Injection Patterns in Svelte

As Svelte applications grow, the need to organize code cleanly becomes more important than simply getting components to work. Real-world applications often rely on shared resources — such as API clients, authentication services, notification handlers, analytics trackers, and configuration settings.

Passing these shared resources through props at every level quickly becomes tedious and messy. Worse, tightly coupling your components directly to global instances makes testing harder, maintenance more fragile, and architecture less flexible.

Dependency Injection (DI) is the practice of **supplying a component with its dependencies from the outside**, rather than hardcoding them inside. While Svelte does not have a built-in DI framework like some other systems, its **Context API** provides all the tools needed to implement clean, effective dependency injection patterns.

At a basic level, dependency injection in Svelte means **providing services or shared objects to components through the Context API**, instead of importing or creating them directly inside each component.

Instead of this tightly coupled pattern:

```
<script>
    import { apiClient } from '../lib/api.js';
</script>

<!-- Component is now hardwired to use a specific
API client -->
```

You move to a pattern where the component asks for its dependency:

```
<script>
    import { getContext } from 'svelte';

    const api = getContext('api');
</script>

<!-- Component works with any API client provided
to it -->
```

This shift means the component is no longer responsible for creating or choosing its dependencies. It simply **uses whatever is provided**, allowing much greater flexibility.

For example:

You can swap implementations easily (e.g., mock APIs for testing)

You can scope different services to different parts of your application

You can reduce unnecessary global imports and side effects

Dependency injection is fundamentally about **separating creation from usage** — and Svelte's Context API makes this straightforward.

Setting Up Dependency Injection Using Context

To inject dependencies in Svelte, you typically define them at a higher-level component — like a layout, page, or provider — and pass them downward through context.

Here's a real-world setup.

Suppose you have an API client:

```
// lib/api.js
export function createApiClient(baseUrl) {
    return {
        async fetchData(endpoint) {
            const res = await
fetch(`${baseUrl}/${endpoint}`);
            if (!res.ok) {
                throw new Error('API error');
            }
            return await res.json();
        }
    };
}
```

You create a provider component:

```
<!-- ApiProvider.svelte -->
<script>
    import { setContext } from 'svelte';
    import { createApiClient } from
'../lib/api.js';

    const api =
createApiClient('https://api.example.com');

    setContext('api', api);
</script>

<slot />
```

This provider sets the `'api'` context key to the API client.

Any child component can now retrieve and use the API without direct imports:

```svelte
<!-- UserList.svelte -->
<script>
    import { getContext } from 'svelte';

    const api = getContext('api');

    let users = [];

    async function loadUsers() {
        users = await api.fetchData('users');
    }
</script>

<button on:click={loadUsers}>
    Load Users
</button>

<ul>
    {#each users as user}
        <li>{user.name}</li>
    {/each}
</ul>
```

This setup has several major advantages:

UserList does not care how api is created.

UserList becomes much easier to test because you can inject a fake or mock api during testing.

You can change the base URL, authentication strategies, or even the API library itself without touching the component.

Injecting Multiple Services

You are not limited to a single injected dependency. You can provide multiple services through context as needed.

Suppose you want to inject an API client, a notification system, and a user session manager.

You could set them like this:

```svelte
<!-- AppProvider.svelte -->
<script>
    import { setContext } from 'svelte';
    import { createApiClient } from
'../lib/api.js';
    import { createNotifier } from
'../lib/notifications.js';
    import { createSessionManager } from
'../lib/session.js';

    setContext('api',
createApiClient('https://api.example.com'));
    setContext('notifier', createNotifier());
    setContext('session', createSessionManager());
</script>

<slot />
```

Then, in any child component, you selectively retrieve only what you need:

```svelte
<script>
    import { getContext } from 'svelte';

    const notifier = getContext('notifier');

    function showWelcomeMessage() {
        notifier.notify('Welcome back!');
    }
</script>

<button on:click={showWelcomeMessage}>
    Greet User
</button>
```

Each service remains modular. Components stay focused and reusable without carrying unnecessary baggage.

This pattern becomes crucial when building large applications where services grow over time — for example, analytics handlers, feature flag managers, logging utilities, etc.

Dependency Injection for Testing and Mocking

One of the most powerful benefits of dependency injection is **testability**.

When components rely on injected dependencies rather than hardcoded imports, you can easily swap in mock versions during tests.

Suppose you have a `UserList.svelte` that uses an injected `api`.

In production, you provide the real API client:

```
<ApiProvider>

    <UserList />

</ApiProvider>
```

During testing, you can provide a mock API:

```
<!-- MockApiProvider.svelte -->
<script>
    import { setContext } from 'svelte';

    const fakeApi = {
        async fetchData(endpoint) {
            if (endpoint === 'users') {
                return [{ name: 'Test User' }];
            }
        }
    };

    setContext('api', fakeApi);
</script>

<slot />
```

Testing then becomes simple:

```
<MockApiProvider>

    <UserList />
```

```
</MockApiProvider>
```

There is no need to modify `UserList.svelte` for tests. It simply uses whatever API client it receives.

This separation is fundamental to writing maintainable, robust code that can be reliably tested in isolation.

Best Practices for Dependency Injection in Svelte

To maximize the benefits of DI patterns in Svelte, keep the following guidelines in mind:

Use consistent context keys. Prefer using imported symbols or constants rather than hardcoded strings to avoid collisions.

Scope dependencies appropriately. Not every service needs to be global. Only inject services at the level where they are truly needed.

Keep providers thin. Providers should focus only on setting up dependencies, not on application logic.

Inject by feature, not by file. If different features need different configurations of a service, provide separate contexts rather than trying to force everything through a single global instance.

Design services to be replaceable. Good services expose clear interfaces, allowing real and fake versions to be easily swapped.

Following these practices helps keep your application clean, modular, scalable, and testable.

Dependency injection patterns in Svelte — powered by Context — give you full control over how shared services flow through your application without hard-coding, over-coupling, or polluting global state.

By injecting services cleanly, you design components that are **smaller**, **more reusable**, **easier to test**, and **easier to extend** over time.

Chapter 5: Structuring Scalable Svelte Projects

When you're building small applications, it's easy to be flexible with structure. You might have a single `src` folder filled with components, stores, utilities, and assets all mixed together. It works because the surface area is small and there aren't too many moving parts to manage.

But as applications grow — especially when teams grow alongside them — the lack of structure starts creating friction. Features become harder to find. Shared utilities get duplicated inconsistently. Refactoring risks breaking unrelated parts of the application. And onboarding new developers becomes slow and painful.

Scalable project structure is not just about being organized. It's about laying down a strong foundation that makes development faster, safer, and more collaborative over time.

Organizing Components, Stores, and Utilities

When you're starting out with a small Svelte project, throwing everything into a single `src` folder seems harmless. A few components here, a store there, a couple of utilities tucked into a corner. It feels manageable.

But once your project grows past a few pages, or once multiple developers start contributing, this casual structure quickly turns into a bottleneck. Features overlap. Shared functions get duplicated. Refactoring becomes risky. Development speed drops because nobody is sure where things should go.

A scalable Svelte project demands a clear, organized structure — not just for today's code, but for tomorrow's features, new teammates, and future maintenance.

Organizing Components for Scalability

In a small project, it's tempting to throw all your `.svelte` files into a single `components/` folder. But this approach doesn't scale. As you add dozens — or hundreds — of components, the flat structure becomes hard to navigate.

A better way to organize components is **by feature or domain**, not by type.

Let's break it down with a working example.

Suppose you're building a dashboard application. Instead of:

```
src/
  components/
    Button.svelte
    Modal.svelte
    Dashboard.svelte
    Chart.svelte
    RevenueSummary.svelte
    Sidebar.svelte
```

you structure it like this:

```
src/
  lib/
    components/
      common/
        Button.svelte
        Modal.svelte
      dashboard/
        DashboardLayout.svelte
        ChartCard.svelte
        RevenueSummary.svelte
        Sidebar.svelte
```

Here's why this is better:

common/ holds truly shared components — buttons, modals, icons, alerts — things that can be reused everywhere.

dashboard/ holds components that belong specifically to the dashboard feature.

When you add new features, like a billing area, you simply create a new `billing/` folder under `components/`.

Each feature owns its own components. You avoid huge folders. You avoid cross-feature pollution. You make maintenance and onboarding dramatically easier.

When working in larger teams, this kind of organization becomes critical: developers immediately know where to find, add, or fix things.

Structuring Stores for Clean State Management

Just like components, your state management needs a structure that grows with your application.

In small apps, you might throw all your stores into a single `store.js` file. It works — until you need multiple stores with different responsibilities.

A clean, scalable structure for stores might look like this:

```
src/
  lib/
    stores/
      authStore.js
      dashboardStore.js
      billingStore.js
      uiStore.js
```

Each store file manages **one feature's or one domain's state**.

For example:

```
// src/lib/stores/authStore.js
import { writable } from 'svelte/store';

export const user = writable(null);
export const isAuthenticated = writable(false);

export function login(userData) {
    user.set(userData);
    isAuthenticated.set(true);
}

export function logout() {
    user.set(null);
    isAuthenticated.set(false);
}
// src/lib/stores/dashboardStore.js
import { writable } from 'svelte/store';

export const dashboardStats = writable([]);
export const loadingDashboard = writable(false);
```

With this structure:

You avoid bloated store files trying to manage unrelated things.

You can focus each store around a clear responsibility.

You make it easy to lazy-load only the stores needed for specific pages, improving performance.

When working on larger applications — especially those using dynamic imports and lazy loading — separating stores by domain becomes essential.

Organizing Utilities and Helper Functions

Utilities are easy to neglect when a project is small. It's common to start writing functions like `formatDate()`, `capitalize()`, and `truncateText()` inside your components or stores.

But this quickly leads to duplication, inconsistencies, and bloated components.

The right approach is to centralize utilities early on.

Structure your utilities like this:

```
src/

  lib/

    utils/

      formatDate.js

      validateEmail.js

      debounce.js

      throttle.js
```
Each utility should **do one thing** and **be reusable across the application**.

Example:

```
// src/lib/utils/formatDate.js
export function formatDate(dateString) {
    const options = { year: 'numeric', month:
'short', day: 'numeric' };
    return new
Date(dateString).toLocaleDateString(undefined,
options);
}
```

Now, wherever you need date formatting, you import it:

```
import { formatDate } from '$lib/utils/formatDate.js';
```

By organizing utilities carefully:

You avoid duplicating small but important functions across files.

You ensure consistent behavior across different parts of the application.

You make utility functions easier to test independently.

Even in very large applications, your `utils/` folder stays manageable if you follow this discipline.

Practical Exercise: Refactoring a Small App for Structure

Suppose you start with a messy small app like this:

```
src/

  App.svelte

  Login.svelte

  Dashboard.svelte

  store.js

  utils.js
```

As it grows, you refactor into a clean structure:

```
src/
  lib/
    components/
      common/
        Button.svelte
        Modal.svelte
      auth/
        LoginForm.svelte
      dashboard/
        DashboardLayout.svelte
        ChartCard.svelte
    stores/
      authStore.js
      dashboardStore.js
    utils/
      formatDate.js
      validateEmail.js
    services/
      apiClient.js
  routes/
    +page.svelte
    dashboard/
      +layout.svelte
      +page.svelte
    login/
      +page.svelte
```

Every piece has a clear place:

Authentication concerns live together (login form, auth store).

Dashboard components and stores are isolated.

Utilities are separated from services.

This kind of refactoring pays off exponentially as the project grows. New features integrate cleanly. Bugs stay localized. Testing becomes easier. Developer productivity stays high.

Organizing your components, stores, and utilities properly is not about adding layers of bureaucracy. It's about **building a structure that stays healthy as your application scales**.

When you group by feature, modularize stores, centralize utilities, and separate business logic from UI, you give your Svelte project the foundation it needs to handle real-world complexity without becoming a tangled mess.

Good structure does not just help today. It ensures your codebase stays fast, understandable, and maintainable six months from now — even when teams grow, features expand, and requirements evolve.

Best Practices for Large Codebases

As Svelte projects grow from hobby experiments to real-world, production-grade applications, the demands on your codebase change drastically. What worked for five components and one page quickly becomes a burden when you are managing dozens of features, multiple developers, and changing business requirements.

A large codebase doesn't just need to work — it needs to be **fast**, **understandable**, **maintainable**, and **safe to modify** over time. Without strong best practices, even well-intentioned teams can find themselves battling technical debt that slows everything down.

Keep Components Small, Focused, and Pure

In large codebases, massive, do-everything components become a major liability. They are harder to read, harder to test, and risk breaking when small changes are made.

The best practice is to design **small, focused, pure components**.

Each component should have a **single responsibility**. If a component starts handling multiple unrelated tasks — for example, displaying a chart, fetching data, and managing user authentication — that's a clear signal it needs to be split.

For instance, instead of a giant `Dashboard.svelte` handling everything, you break it cleanly:

```
<!-- DashboardLayout.svelte -->

<ChartCard />

<RevenueSummary />

<ActivityFeed />
```

Each subcomponent (`ChartCard.svelte`, `RevenueSummary.svelte`, `ActivityFeed.svelte`) handles one specific piece of the UI.

Small, pure components:

Are easier to read at a glance

Can be tested independently

Encourage better reusability

Reduce the blast radius when bugs appear

If a component starts creeping past 150–200 lines, review it carefully. It may be time to refactor.

Strictly Separate Business Logic from UI

Keeping business logic inside UI components is manageable at first, but over time it becomes a trap. Components should focus on **how** data is presented, not **where** it comes from or **how** it is processed.

All heavy logic — such as data fetching, validation, transformation, or service interaction — should live inside:

Stores

Utilities

Services

For example, in an authentication feature, your login form component should be thin:

```
<script>
    import { authStore } from
'$lib/stores/authStore.js';

    let email = '';
    let password = '';

    async function submit() {
        await authStore.login(email, password);
    }
</script>

<form on:submit|preventDefault={submit}>
    <input bind:value={email} type="email"
placeholder="Email" />
    <input bind:value={password} type="password"
placeholder="Password" />
    <button type="submit">Login</button>
</form>
```

The heavy lifting happens inside the store:

```
// src/lib/stores/authStore.js
import { writable } from 'svelte/store';
import { apiClient } from
'$lib/services/apiClient.js';

export const user = writable(null);
export const isAuthenticated = writable(false);

export async function login(email, password) {
    const response = await
apiClient.post('/login', { email, password });

    user.set(response.user);

    isAuthenticated.set(true);
}
```

This separation makes your components easier to understand and your business logic easier to test and reuse across multiple components.

Prefer Feature-Based Folder Structure

In small projects, grouping by type (all components together, all stores together) seems clean. But in large codebases, this leads to friction, because features cut across types.

It is better to group **by feature** instead.

Structure your project like this:

```
src/

  lib/

    features/

      auth/

        LoginForm.svelte

        SignupForm.svelte

        authStore.js

        authService.js

      dashboard/

        DashboardLayout.svelte

        ChartCard.svelte

        dashboardStore.js

      billing/

        BillingSummary.svelte

        billingStore.js

    components/
```

```
common/

    Button.svelte

    Modal.svelte

utils/

    formatDate.js

services/

    apiClient.js
```

Each feature owns its components, stores, and services. Common/shared elements like buttons or modals live in a separate shared area.

This structure:

Improves discoverability

Makes feature development and refactoring isolated and safer

Supports scaling to very large projects

Organizing by feature reflects the mental model of how developers actually work: they think in terms of features, not file types.

Use Explicit Import Paths and Aliases

When applications get big, relative imports like this become confusing:

```
import Modal from '../../../components/common/Modal.svelte';
```

SvelteKit allows you to configure **path aliases** for clean, readable imports.

In `svelte.config.js`, you set up:

```
import { vitePreprocess } from
'@sveltejs/kit/vite';
import path from 'path';

export default {
    preprocess: vitePreprocess(),
    kit: {
        alias: {
```

```
                $components:
path.resolve('./src/lib/components'),
                $stores:
path.resolve('./src/lib/stores'),
                $utils:
path.resolve('./src/lib/utils'),
                $services:
path.resolve('./src/lib/services')
        }
    }
};
```

Now you can import like this:

```
import Modal from
'$components/common/Modal.svelte';

import { authStore } from '$stores/authStore.js';
```

This:

Makes imports shorter and easier to manage

Avoids fragile, deep relative paths

Improves refactoring safety when moving files

Small improvements like this have a huge cumulative impact in large codebases.

Automate Code Quality and Formatting

Large codebases decay quickly without consistent code style enforcement.

Set up:

Prettier for consistent formatting (indentation, quotes, semicolons)

ESLint for catching common JavaScript mistakes

Stylelint for CSS and styling consistency

In SvelteKit projects, you can easily configure Prettier:

```
npm install --save-dev prettier prettier-plugin-svelte
```

Then create a `.prettierrc` file:

```
{

    "semi": true,

    "singleQuote": true,

    "svelteSortOrder": "scripts-markup-styles",

    "svelteStrictMode": true,

    "svelteBracketNewLine": true,

    "svelteAllowShorthand": false

}
```

Hook Prettier into your workflow:

Pre-commit hooks (with tools like Husky and lint-staged)

CI pipelines that enforce formatting before merging

Consistency reduces noise in code reviews and improves collaboration across teams.

Document Shared APIs and Store Contracts

In large applications, shared services and stores become public APIs that many developers depend on. Changes to these without clear communication can introduce bugs.

A practical solution is lightweight documentation:

Each store or service file should have a clear comment describing its public methods and expected usage.

If the store has complex behavior, briefly document how subscriptions and updates work.

Example in `authStore.js`:

```
/**
```

```
 * authStore
 *
 * - user: writable(null) — Current authenticated
user
 * - isAuthenticated: writable(false) — Boolean
login state
 * - login(email, password): Promise<void> —
Authenticate a user
 * - logout(): void — Clear authentication
 */
```

Clear documentation:

Improves onboarding for new developers

Reduces accidental misuse of shared code

Makes future refactoring less dangerous

Maintaining a healthy large codebase is not about adding layers of complexity. It's about applying **simple, consistent, practical best practices** that keep complexity under control.

By keeping components small and pure, separating logic from UI, structuring by feature, enforcing code quality, using explicit imports, and documenting shared APIs clearly, you create a project that stays fast, clean, and easy to extend — even as it grows from dozens to hundreds of modules.

Working with Monorepos and Shared Libraries

As Svelte projects mature, it becomes common to build not just a single application, but an ecosystem of related apps. You might start with a customer-facing dashboard, later add an admin panel, then a marketing website, then internal tools — all needing to share components, utilities, and services.

Managing these separate codebases individually quickly turns into a problem:

Shared components get copied instead of reused.

Fixing a bug in one app does not fix it in others.

Updates become inconsistent, increasing maintenance cost.

The professional solution is to move toward a **monorepo** setup with **shared libraries**. This structure keeps everything organized, accelerates development, and reduces duplication without adding unnecessary complexity.

Understanding Monorepo

A **monorepo** (short for "monolithic repository") is a single Git repository that contains **multiple related applications** and **shared code packages**.

Instead of having:

`customer-dashboard` in one repo

`admin-panel` in another repo

`marketing-site` in a third repo

You have one repository structured like:

```
apps/
   customer-dashboard/
   admin-panel/
   marketing-site/
packages/
   ui-library/
   core-services/
   shared-utils/
```

Each app is a separate project that can be built and deployed independently. Each package is a reusable library that apps can import.

This approach:

Improves code sharing

Reduces duplicated logic

Simplifies updates across apps

Enables unified version control and testing

Modern tooling like **pnpm workspaces**, **TurboRepo**, or **Nx** makes monorepo management smooth and efficient, even for very large projects.

Structuring a Svelte Monorepo

A practical and scalable layout for a Svelte monorepo looks like this:

```
apps/
  customer-dashboard/
    svelte.config.js
    src/
      lib/
        components/
        stores/
        utils/
      routes/
  admin-panel/
    svelte.config.js
    src/
      lib/
        components/
        stores/
        utils/
      routes/
  marketing-site/
    svelte.config.js
    src/
      lib/
        components/
        stores/
        utils/
      routes/
packages/
  ui-library/
```

```
      src/
         Button.svelte
         Modal.svelte
         Card.svelte
   core-services/
      src/
         apiClient.js
         authService.js
   shared-utils/
      src/
         formatDate.js
         capitalize.js
pnpm-workspace.yaml
package.json
tsconfig.base.json
```

apps/ contains your applications.

packages/ contains your reusable libraries:

`ui-library/` — reusable Svelte components shared across apps

`core-services/` — API clients, authentication, notification handlers

`shared-utils/` — common helper functions like formatting dates or numbers

Each project can have its own `svelte.config.js` tuned to its needs, but they share the same TypeScript base config if you are using TypeScript.

Each app can import shared libraries easily using workspace aliases like:

```
import { Button } from '@myorg/ui-library';

import { apiClient } from '@myorg/core-services';

import { formatDate } from '@myorg/shared-utils';
```

This setup makes the boundary between shared code and application-specific code clear and intentional.

Setting Up a Svelte Monorepo with pnpm Workspaces

pnpm is a modern, efficient package manager that handles workspaces very well. Setting up a monorepo with pnpm is straightforward.

First, create a `pnpm-workspace.yaml` at the root of your repository:

```
packages:
  - apps/*
  - packages/*
```

This tells pnpm to treat everything under `apps/` and `packages/` as workspace packages.

Your root `package.json` should look like:

```
{
  "name": "my-monorepo",
  "private": true,
  "workspaces": [
    "apps/*",
    "packages/*"
  ],
  "scripts": {
    "dev:dashboard": "pnpm --filter customer-dashboard dev",
    "dev:admin": "pnpm --filter admin-panel dev",
    "build:all": "pnpm --filter ./... build"
  },
  "devDependencies": {
    "svelte": "^4.0.0",
    "svelte-kit": "next",
    "vite": "^5.0.0"
  }
}
```

Now, inside any app (like `customer-dashboard`), you can add local dependencies:

```
pnpm add @myorg/ui-library @myorg/core-services
```

pnpm links these packages automatically using symlinks, meaning no need for separate npm publishing or manual file copying during development.

Building and Importing Shared Libraries

Inside each package like `ui-library`, set up a basic `package.json`:

```json
{

  "name": "@myorg/ui-library",

  "version": "0.0.1",

  "svelte": "./src/index.js",

  "exports": {

    ".": "./src/index.js"

  }

}
```

Your `src/index.js` should export everything you want to share:

```js
export { default as Button } from
'./Button.svelte';

export { default as Modal } from './Modal.svelte';

export { default as Card } from './Card.svelte';
```

Now in any app, you can use the shared library cleanly:

```svelte
<script>
    import { Button, Modal } from '@myorg/ui-
library';
</script>

<Button>Submit</Button>
<Modal title="Example Modal" />
```

You can build shared packages separately if needed, but during development, pnpm's symlinks mean everything stays live and up-to-date.

Practical Example: Fixing a Bug Across All Apps

Suppose you find a bug in the `Button.svelte` component inside `ui-library`.

Instead of hunting down copies of the Button component across multiple apps, you:

Fix `Button.svelte` inside `packages/ui-library/src/Button.svelte`

Bump the version if needed

Apps using `@myorg/ui-library` automatically get the update

You fix the problem once. Every app benefits immediately.

This process:

Reduces duplication

Improves consistency

Speeds up bugfixes and new feature rollouts

Reduces maintenance cost dramatically

In fast-moving projects, this advantage cannot be overstated.

Working with monorepos and shared libraries is not just about keeping code organized. It's about enabling **faster iteration**, **easier maintenance**, **consistent user experience**, and **professional-level collaboration** across multiple Svelte applications.

By structuring your projects cleanly around apps and packages, using modern tools like pnpm workspaces, and thinking modularly about shared code, you prepare your Svelte ecosystem to grow naturally without drowning in technical debt.

Chapter 6: Handling Asynchronous Workflows

Modern web applications live and breathe on asynchronous operations. Whether it's loading user data, submitting forms, fetching analytics, or syncing real-time updates, handling asynchronous workflows properly is fundamental to delivering fast, responsive, and reliable user experiences.

In Svelte applications, managing asynchronous workflows goes beyond calling `fetch()` and showing a loading spinner. At scale, you need structured strategies for **data fetching**, **caching**, **progressive rendering**, **streaming**, and **gracefully handling errors and load states** — all without slowing down your interface or confusing your users.

Strategies for Async Data Fetching and Caching

When you start building applications with Svelte, working with asynchronous data usually begins with a simple `fetch()` inside a component. For small prototypes, that's enough. But as your application grows, so does the complexity around loading data: you need to handle retries, loading states, caching, optimistic updates, and minimize redundant network requests.

Properly structuring **async data fetching and caching** is crucial for building applications that feel responsive, efficient, and professional.

Let's begin by considering the **baseline**: fetching data cleanly and explicitly handling the loading, success, and error states.

Instead of hiding fetching logic deep inside a component, you create **dedicated services** or **API modules**.

Start with an API client abstraction:

```
// src/lib/services/apiClient.js
export async function fetchData(endpoint, options =
{}) {
    const response = await fetch(endpoint,
options);
```

```
    if (!response.ok) {
        throw new Error(`Failed to fetch
${endpoint}: ${response.statusText}`);
    }

    return await response.json();
}
```

This separates the concern of making HTTP requests from the components that use the data.

Then inside your Svelte component:

```
<script>
    import { fetchData } from
'$lib/services/apiClient.js';

    let items = [];
    let loading = false;
    let error = null;

    async function loadItems() {
        loading = true;
        error = null;

        try {
            items = await
fetchData('/api/items');
        } catch (err) {
            error = err.message || 'Unknown
error';
        } finally {
            loading = false;
        }
    }
</script>

{#if loading}
    <p>Loading items...</p>
{:else if error}
    <p>Error: {error}</p>
{:else if items.length}
    <ul>
```

```
        {#each items as item}
            <li>{item.name}</li>
        {/each}
    </ul>
{:else}
    <p>No items available.</p>
{/if}

<button on:click={loadItems}>Refresh Items</button>
```

This clean structure allows:

A clear loading indicator.

A clear error message if the fetch fails.

Separation between the fetching mechanism and the UI.

Already, this is far more maintainable than mixing `fetch()` and JSX logic in the same place.

Implementing Simple In-Memory Caching

Once you have stable fetching logic, you can improve performance by **caching** the results — especially for endpoints that don't change frequently, like user profiles or product lists.

You can extend your API client to include an in-memory cache:

```
// src/lib/services/apiClient.js
const cache = new Map();

export async function fetchDataCached(endpoint,
options = {}) {
    if (cache.has(endpoint)) {
        return cache.get(endpoint);
    }

    const response = await fetch(endpoint,
options);

    if (!response.ok) {
        throw new Error(`Failed to fetch
${endpoint}: ${response.statusText}`);
```

```
    }

    const data = await response.json();
    cache.set(endpoint, data);
    return data;
}
```

Now your fetching becomes cache-aware automatically.

In the component:

```
<script>
    import { fetchDataCached } from
'$lib/services/apiClient.js';

    let user = null;
    let loading = false;
    let error = null;

    async function loadUser() {
        loading = true;
        error = null;

        try {
            user = await
fetchDataCached('/api/user');
        } catch (err) {
            error = err.message || 'Unable to
load user';
        } finally {
            loading = false;
        }
    }
</script>

{#if loading}
    <p>Loading user information...</p>
{:else if error}
    <p>Error: {error}</p>
{:else if user}
    <p>Welcome, {user.name}</p>
{/if}
```

```
<button on:click={loadUser}>Refresh User
Info</button>
```

Using simple in-memory caching:

Reduces repeated network requests when data is stable.

Improves perceived performance for users.

Minimizes server load and bandwidth usage.

For most public data APIs that don't change often (like product categories, countries, settings), this is enough.

Handling Cache Invalidation and Revalidation

Caching is helpful, but stale data can become a problem. You need strategies for **invalidating** or **revalidating** cached data when necessary.

You can extend your `fetchDataCached` with manual cache invalidation:

```
export function invalidateCache(endpoint) {
     cache.delete(endpoint);
}
```

Now in your component or service logic, if you know the data has changed (for example, after submitting a form that updates the user), you can invalidate the relevant cache:

```
<script>
     import { fetchDataCached, invalidateCache }
from '$lib/services/apiClient.js';

     async function refreshUser() {
          invalidateCache('/api/user');
          await loadUser();
     }
</script>
```

This gives you fine-grained control:

Only invalidate what you need.

Avoid unnecessary reloads elsewhere.

Keep the rest of the application fast.

In more advanced setups, you can even set cache expiration timers:

```
const cacheExpiry = new Map();

export async function
fetchDataCachedWithTTL(endpoint, ttl = 30000) {
    const now = Date.now();

    if (cache.has(endpoint) && now <
(cacheExpiry.get(endpoint) || 0)) {
            return cache.get(endpoint);
    }

    const response = await fetch(endpoint);

    if (!response.ok) {
            throw new Error(`Failed to fetch
${endpoint}`);
    }

    const data = await response.json();
    cache.set(endpoint, data);
    cacheExpiry.set(endpoint, now + ttl);
    return data;
}
```

Now, cached entries expire automatically after `ttl` milliseconds.

This pattern — **stale-while-revalidate** — is common in production systems, balancing freshness and performance.

Real-World Example: Data Fetching with SvelteKit Load Functions

In SvelteKit, you can fetch data server-side inside `+page.js` or `+page.server.js` files, improving both SEO and performance.

Example +page.js:

```
// src/routes/dashboard/+page.js
import { fetchData } from
'$lib/services/apiClient.js';

export async function load() {
    const stats = await
fetchData('/api/dashboard/stats');
    return { stats };
}
```

In your `DashboardPage.svelte`:

```
<script>
    export let data;
</script>

<h1>Dashboard Stats</h1>

<ul>
    {#each data.stats as stat}
        <li>{stat.label}: {stat.value}</li>
    {/each}
</ul>
```

Because the data is fetched inside the `load` function, it:

Happens before the page is rendered.

Reduces "loading flash" when transitioning between pages.

Allows SvelteKit to optimize preloading and caching at the framework level.

Using SvelteKit's load system properly means you don't have to manage loading states manually for every page — a major advantage for larger applications.

Handling asynchronous data fetching and caching in Svelte requires careful structure, not improvisation. By creating dedicated services for fetching, explicitly managing loading and error states, implementing in-memory caching, handling cache invalidation thoughtfully, and leveraging framework features like `load()` in SvelteKit, you create applications that feel fast, predictable, and professional.

These are the building blocks that allow your apps to scale gracefully, even under demanding real-world conditions — with thousands of users, unstable networks, and constantly changing data.

Progressive Rendering and Streaming Techniques

In web development, speed is not just about how fast your server responds — it's about how quickly your users start seeing and interacting with useful content. Even if your backend takes a second or two to fetch all the required data, you should never let your users stare at a blank page during that wait.

This is where **progressive rendering** and **streaming techniques** come into play.

Instead of waiting for all data to be ready before rendering anything, you **progressively display parts of the interface** as soon as possible, while other parts continue loading in the background.

This approach dramatically improves **perceived performance**, keeps users engaged, and makes your applications feel faster, even when dealing with large datasets or slow network conditions.

What Progressive Rendering Means in Svelte

Progressive rendering in Svelte means **building your pages and components so that each section can load independently**, rather than locking the entire page behind a single fetch.

Rather than designing your page as:

Fetch everything

Then render the page

you build it as:

Render skeleton or placeholder content immediately

Fetch and populate sections asynchronously as each piece becomes ready

This way:

Users immediately see structure, navigation, headers, and interactive elements

Only individual sections show loading states

The app stays responsive during data loading

Structuring Components for Progressive Loading

A key strategy for progressive rendering is **breaking large pages into smaller, independently loading components**.

Instead of doing this inside one large page:

```
<script>
    const user = await fetchUser();
    const stats = await fetchStats();
    const notifications = await
fetchNotifications();
</script>

<Layout>
    <UserProfile {user} />
    <DashboardStats {stats} />
    <Notifications {notifications} />
</Layout>
```

you restructure your page like this:

```
<script>

    // No blocking awaits here

</script>


<Layout>

    <UserProfileLoader />

    <DashboardStatsLoader />

    <NotificationsLoader />

</Layout>
```

Each of those `Loader` components becomes responsible for fetching its own data and managing its own loading, success, and error states internally.

Example for `UserProfileLoader.svelte`:

```
<script>
     import { fetchUser } from
'$lib/services/apiClient.js';
     import { onMount } from 'svelte';

     let user = null;
     let loading = true;
     let error = null;

     onMount(async () => {
          try {
               user = await fetchUser();
          } catch (err) {
               error = err.message || 'Failed to
load user';
          } finally {
               loading = false;
          }
     });
</script>

{#if loading}
     <p>Loading user info...</p>
{:else if error}
     <p>Error loading user: {error}</p>
{:else}
     <section class="user-profile">
          <h2>{user.name}</h2>
          <p>{user.email}</p>
     </section>
{/if}
```

Now:

`UserProfileLoader` shows immediately, even if it's just a spinner.

`DashboardStatsLoader` and `NotificationsLoader` can fetch in parallel.

Sections update independently as their data becomes available.

The user never sees a blank page. They see progressive construction of content — which feels dramatically faster.

Skeleton Screens: Improving Perceived Speed

One simple but highly effective enhancement for progressive rendering is **skeleton screens** — empty or greyed-out UI elements that hint at the structure of the page while real data loads.

Instead of showing a generic spinner, you sketch out what the content will look like.

Example inside `UserProfileLoader.svelte`:

```
{#if loading}
    <div class="skeleton-profile">
        <div class="avatar-placeholder"></div>
        <div class="text-placeholder"></div>
        <div class="text-placeholder"></div>
    </div>
{:else if error}
    <p>Error loading user: {error}</p>
{:else}
    <section class="user-profile">
        <h2>{user.name}</h2>
        <p>{user.email}</p>
    </section>
{/if}
```

CSS:

```
.skeleton-profile {
    display: flex;
    flex-direction: column;
    gap: 8px;
}
.avatar-placeholder {
    width: 50px;
    height: 50px;
    background-color: #ccc;
    border-radius: 50%;
```

```
}
.text-placeholder {
    width: 100%;
    height: 16px;
    background-color: #ccc;
    border-radius: 4px;
}
```

Skeleton screens:

Keep the layout stable (no sudden jumps)

Give users a visual cue about what's coming

Make the application feel faster and more polished

In modern UI/UX design, skeleton screens are now a baseline expectation for professional applications.

Streaming Data in SvelteKit

While progressive rendering improves perceived speed, **streaming** can optimize **actual** delivery time — by sending parts of a page to the browser as soon as they are ready, instead of waiting for the whole page.

SvelteKit supports **partial responses** using endpoint handlers.

You can design API endpoints that stream responses using **ReadableStream**.

Here's a simple example of creating a streaming endpoint:

```
// src/routes/api/stream-data/+server.js
export async function GET() {
    const encoder = new TextEncoder();
    const stream = new ReadableStream({
        start(controller) {

    controller.enqueue(encoder.encode('First
chunk\n'));

            setTimeout(() => {

    controller.enqueue(encoder.encode('Second
chunk\n'));
```

```
            controller.close();
        }, 1000);
    }
});

return new Response(stream, {
    headers: { 'Content-Type': 'text/plain' }
});
}
```

In the client, you can consume the stream:

```
const response = await fetch('/api/stream-data');
const reader = response.body.getReader();
const decoder = new TextDecoder();

let done = false;
while (!done) {
    const { value, done: readerDone } = await
reader.read();
    if (value) {
        console.log(decoder.decode(value));
    }
    done = readerDone;
}
```

This approach:

Sends first meaningful content immediately.

Streams large or slow-loading content piece-by-piece.

Improves time-to-first-byte and interactive readiness.

While streaming is an advanced technique, it becomes essential when building real-time dashboards, live feeds, chat applications, or data-heavy analytic systems.

Real-World Exercise: Progressive Dashboard Layout

Suppose you're building a user dashboard that shows:

Profile Information

Recent Activity

Notifications

Billing Summary

Instead of fetching everything upfront, structure the page:

```
<ProfileLoader />

<ActivityFeedLoader />

<NotificationsLoader />

<BillingSummaryLoader />
```

Each loader:

Fetches its own data

Shows its own skeleton or loading indicator

Handles its own errors independently

Benefits:

Users see the dashboard frame immediately.

Each piece loads and populates independently, as soon as it's ready.

A failure in one section (for example, billing service down) does not break the rest of the dashboard.

This is progressive rendering at work — and it makes a real, measurable difference in how users perceive the speed and reliability of your application.

Progressive rendering and streaming are no longer luxury features reserved for giant tech companies. They are **practical, necessary strategies** for building modern web applications that feel fast, responsive, and robust — even under challenging network or backend conditions.

By structuring your components independently, managing loading states carefully, using skeleton screens for polished UX, and implementing streaming where appropriate, you build applications that not only perform better but **feel dramatically faster** to users.

Managing Errors and Loading States

In real-world applications, asynchronous operations like data fetching, form submissions, or file uploads can fail for many reasons — network issues, server errors, invalid data, user interruptions, and more.

Professional-grade applications are not judged by how often they fail — they are judged by **how well they handle failure**.

Managing **errors** and **loading states** gracefully is critical for creating user experiences that feel reliable, trustworthy, and polished. Users need to know exactly what's happening, whether the system is loading, succeeded, or encountered a problem — without confusion, frustration, or guesswork.

Handling Loading States Explicitly

Whenever your application triggers an asynchronous action, you should always provide **immediate visual feedback** to the user that something is happening.

A loading state should:

Be visually distinct from both success and error states

Appear instantly when the action starts

Disappear immediately once the action completes or fails

Let's build a clear structure.

Suppose you have a button that fetches user data:

```
<script>
    import { fetchData } from
'$lib/services/apiClient.js';

    let user = null;
    let loading = false;
    let error = null;

    async function loadUser() {
        loading = true;
        error = null;
```

```
        try {
                user = await fetchData('/api/user');
        } catch (err) {
                error = err.message || 'Failed to
load user';
        } finally {
                loading = false;
        }
    }
</script>

{#if loading}
    <p>Loading user information...</p>
{:else if error}
    <p class="error">Error: {error}</p>
{:else if user}
    <section>
            <h2>{user.name}</h2>
            <p>{user.email}</p>
    </section>
{/if}

<button on:click={loadUser} disabled={loading}>
    {loading ? 'Loading...' : 'Load User'}
</button>
```

In this structure:

The `loading` variable controls whether to show a spinner, skeleton, or disabled button.

Button text changes dynamically during the load.

The button is disabled while loading to prevent double submissions.

This pattern gives users immediate, responsive feedback that **something is happening** after their action, even before the data is available.

Graceful Error Handling: Making Failure Clear but Friendly

When things go wrong — and they will — you should display **clear, respectful, and actionable** error feedback.

Good error handling:

Clearly states that something failed

Gives a hint about why (if known)

Offers an obvious path forward (retry, refresh, contact support)

Never leave users staring at a broken or frozen page without explanation.

Expanding the previous example:

```
{#if loading}
    <p>Loading user information...</p>
{:else if error}
    <div class="error-message">
        <p>Oops! {error}</p>
        <button
on:click={loadUser}>Retry</button>
    </div>
{:else if user}
    <section>
        <h2>{user.name}</h2>
        <p>{user.email}</p>
    </section>
{/if}
```

Key points:

Show the error clearly.

Offer a **Retry** button immediately.

Allow the user to recover without needing to refresh the page manually.

Do not bury errors in the console. Users don't open DevTools to figure out why their dashboard didn't load.

Do not hide error states behind infinite spinners. Infinite loading without feedback looks like a broken application.

Building Reusable Error and Loading Components

When building larger applications, writing the same `{#if loading}{:else if error}{:else}` blocks everywhere becomes repetitive.

A better approach is to abstract loading and error UI into **reusable components**.

Create a reusable `AsyncWrapper.svelte`:

```svelte
<script>
    export let loading = false;
    export let error = null;
    export let onRetry;
</script>

{#if loading}
    <div class="loading-spinner">Loading...</div>
{:else if error}
    <div class="error-state">
        <p>{error}</p>
        {#if onRetry}
            <button
on:click={onRetry}>Retry</button>
        {/if}
    </div>
{:else}
    <slot />
{/if}
```

Then use it like this inside your real components:

```svelte
<script>
    import { fetchData } from
'$lib/services/apiClient.js';
    import AsyncWrapper from
'$lib/components/common/AsyncWrapper.svelte';

    let profile = null;
    let loading = false;
    let error = null;

    async function loadProfile() {
        loading = true;
        error = null;

        try {
```

```
                profile = await
fetchData('/api/profile');
        } catch (err) {
                error = err.message || 'Could not
load profile';
        } finally {
                loading = false;
        }
    }
</script>

<AsyncWrapper {loading} {error}
onRetry={loadProfile}>
    <section>
            <h2>{profile.name}</h2>
            <p>{profile.email}</p>
    </section>
</AsyncWrapper>

<button on:click={loadProfile} disabled={loading}>
    {loading ? 'Loading...' : 'Load Profile'}
</button>
```

By reusing `AsyncWrapper`, your code stays clean, consistent, and easier to maintain.

This also allows you to style and polish loading and error states consistently across the entire application.

Providing Contextual Loading Indicators

Sometimes, showing a full-page loading spinner isn't necessary. Instead, you can show **local loading indicators** tied to specific UI elements.

For example, inside a dashboard with several panels:

```
<Panel title="Recent Activity">
    {#if loadingActivity}
            <ActivitySkeleton />
    {:else if activityError}
            <ErrorMessage message={activityError}
onRetry={loadActivity} />
    {:else}
            <ActivityFeed items={activityItems} />
```

113

```
    {/if}
</Panel>

<Panel title="Billing Overview">
    {#if loadingBilling}
        <BillingSkeleton />
    {:else if billingError}
        <ErrorMessage message={billingError}
onRetry={loadBilling} />
    {:else}
        <BillingSummary data={billingData} />
    {/if}
</Panel>
```

Here:

Each panel handles its own loading and error states independently.

The rest of the dashboard remains visible and usable even if one panel is loading or has failed.

Users feel that the system is **partially available** instead of completely broken.

Handling loading and error states at the **component scope** — not just globally — is a hallmark of polished, high-quality applications.

Best Practices Checklist for Managing Loading and Errors

When designing loading and error management in Svelte apps, always follow these principles:

Immediate Feedback: Always show something instantly when an action starts.

Local Context: Handle loading and errors where they occur, not globally unless necessary.

Clear Messages: Avoid vague errors like "Something went wrong." Be specific whenever possible.

Recovery Options: Always provide retry or refresh options after failures.

Non-Blocking UX: Never block the entire page unless absolutely necessary. Progressive, sectioned loading is better.

Polished Placeholders: Use skeleton screens or subtle spinners to maintain layout stability during loading.

These are the habits that differentiate amateur apps from professional, production-grade software.

Gracefully managing errors and loading states is not just about technical correctness. It's about designing experiences that make users feel informed, respected, and confident even when things go wrong.

By showing loading indicators promptly, handling errors visibly and kindly, offering clear paths to recovery, and keeping your interfaces responsive even during data operations, you build Svelte applications that feel trustworthy, polished, and robust — no matter how complex the underlying workflows.

Chapter 7: Testing and Debugging Svelte Applications

As your Svelte application grows from simple pages to a real product, it becomes critical to move beyond manual testing. Clicking through the interface after every change is slow, error-prone, and unsustainable. Professional development requires **structured, automated testing** and **effective debugging tools** to ensure that your application behaves correctly, remains fast, and can evolve safely.

In this chapter, we will work through **unit testing components with Vitest**, **end-to-end testing with Playwright**, and **debugging reactive state and performance issues**. You'll learn not just how to test, but how to test properly — focusing on techniques that catch real bugs without slowing you down or bloating your workflow.

Unit Testing Components with Vitest

When you're building Svelte components that interact with data, user inputs, and asynchronous operations, manual testing only gets you so far. Clicking through the interface after each change doesn't scale, and it's impossible to catch every edge case by hand.

Unit testing solves this.
It lets you **automatically verify** that your components behave as intended — consistently, efficiently, and safely — even as your codebase evolves.

For Svelte projects, **Vitest** is the best choice for unit testing. It's fast, lightweight, fully Vite-compatible, and integrates naturally into the way SvelteKit applications are built.

Setting Up Vitest for a Svelte Project

To start using Vitest in your project, you first install the necessary packages:

```
npm install --save-dev vitest @testing-
library/svelte @testing-library/jest-dom svelte-
vitest
```

This gives you:

Vitest — the test runner.

Testing Library for Svelte — to render components and simulate user interactions.

Jest DOM matchers — for cleaner, more expressive assertions.

Next, configure `vite.config.js` to enable Vitest:

```
import { sveltekit } from '@sveltejs/kit/vite';
import { defineConfig } from 'vite';

export default defineConfig({
    plugins: [sveltekit()],
    test: {
        include:
['src/**/*.{test,spec}.{js,ts}'],
        environment: 'jsdom'
    }
});
```

By setting `environment: 'jsdom'`, you enable a DOM-like environment, allowing your tests to simulate browser behavior.

Now you're ready to write your first component tests.

Writing a Basic Component Test

Let's start simple.
Suppose you have a basic button component:

```
<!-- src/lib/components/Button.svelte -->
<script>
    export let label = 'Click me';
</script>

<button>{label}</button>
```

You want to test that the button renders with the correct label.

Here's how you write a unit test:

```
// src/lib/components/Button.test.js
import { render } from '@testing-library/svelte';
```

```
import { expect, test } from 'vitest';
import Button from './Button.svelte';

test('renders button with correct label', () => {
    const { getByText } = render(Button, { props:
{ label: 'Submit' } });

    expect(getByText('Submit')).toBeTruthy();
});
```

Let's break this down carefully:

render() mounts the Button component inside a virtual DOM.

{ props: { label: 'Submit' } } sets the label prop.

getByText('Submit') searches for a button with the text Submit.

expect(...).toBeTruthy() asserts that the button actually exists in the DOM.

To run the test:

npx vitest run

If everything is working, you'll see the test pass — verifying that your button correctly renders the provided label.

This is **unit testing at its simplest**: verifying a small, isolated behavior of a single component.

Testing User Interactions

Static rendering tests are useful, but many components have dynamic behavior — clicking, typing, submitting forms.

Testing user interactions involves:

Rendering the component

Firing DOM events (like clicks, inputs)

Asserting changes to the DOM or component state

Let's test a simple counter button:

118

```
<!-- src/lib/components/Counter.svelte -->
<script>
    let count = 0;

    function increment() {
        count += 1;
    }
</script>

<button on:click={increment}>
    Clicked {count} {count === 1 ? 'time' :
'times'}
</button>
```

The button increments a counter every time it's clicked.

Test:

```
// src/lib/components/Counter.test.js
import { render, fireEvent } from '@testing-
library/svelte';
import { expect, test } from 'vitest';
import Counter from './Counter.svelte';

test('increments count on click', async () => {
    const { getByText } = render(Counter);

    const button = getByText('Clicked 0 times');

    await fireEvent.click(button);
    expect(getByText('Clicked 1
time')).toBeTruthy();

    await fireEvent.click(button);
    expect(getByText('Clicked 2
times')).toBeTruthy();
});
```

Here:

`fireEvent.click(button)` simulates a user click.

After each click, you check the updated button text.

Notice: Testing UI interaction **always focuses on visible behavior**, not on internal implementation details.

You're not checking if `count++` was called — you're checking that the user sees the correct information after interacting. This keeps your tests **aligned with real user behavior**.

Testing Event Dispatching

Svelte components often emit custom events. Testing that your component correctly dispatches these events is just as important.

Suppose you have a `LoginForm.svelte`:

```
<script>
    import { createEventDispatcher } from
'svelte';
    const dispatch = createEventDispatcher();

    let email = '';
    let password = '';

    function submitForm() {
        dispatch('submit', { email, password });
    }
</script>

<form on:submit|preventDefault={submitForm}>
    <input bind:value={email} placeholder="Email"
/>
    <input type="password" bind:value={password}
placeholder="Password" />
    <button type="submit">Login</button>
</form>
```

You want to test that:

When the user fills out the form and submits, the `submit` event is fired with the correct data.

Test:

```js
// src/lib/components/LoginForm.test.js
import { render, fireEvent } from '@testing-
library/svelte';
import { expect, test } from 'vitest';
import LoginForm from './LoginForm.svelte';

test('emits submit event with email and password',
async () => {
    const { getByPlaceholderText, getByText,
component } = render(LoginForm);

    const emailInput =
getByPlaceholderText('Email');
    const passwordInput =
getByPlaceholderText('Password');
    const submitButton = getByText('Login');

    await fireEvent.input(emailInput, { target: {
value: 'test@example.com' } });
    await fireEvent.input(passwordInput, { target:
{ value: 'password123' } });

    let eventData;
    component.$on('submit', (event) => {
        eventData = event.detail;
    });

    await fireEvent.submit(submitButton);

    expect(eventData).toEqual({ email:
'test@example.com', password: 'password123' });
});
```

The process:

Simulate input events to type into the form.

Attach an event listener to the component to capture the dispatched event.

Fire the form submit event.

Assert that the dispatched event has the correct payload.

This validates that your **event communication** between components is working correctly.

Mocking External Dependencies

Sometimes, your components depend on external services — like APIs, stores, or context values.

When testing, you want to **mock** these dependencies so your tests stay focused and deterministic.

Suppose your `UserProfile.svelte` loads user info from a store:

```
<script>
    import { user } from
'$lib/stores/userStore.js';
    $: userData = $user;
</script>

{#if userData}
    <h1>{userData.name}</h1>
{:else}
    <p>Loading user...</p>
{/if}
```

You don't want to hit a real API during tests. Instead, you mock the store:

```
// src/lib/components/UserProfile.test.js
import { render } from '@testing-library/svelte';
import { writable } from 'svelte/store';
import { expect, test, vi } from 'vitest';
import UserProfile from './UserProfile.svelte';

// Mock userStore
vi.mock('$lib/stores/userStore.js', () => {
    const user = writable({ name: 'Jane Doe' });
    return { user };
});

test('renders user name', () => {
    const { getByText } = render(UserProfile);
    expect(getByText('Jane Doe')).toBeTruthy();
```

```
 });
```

Using `vi.mock()`, you replace the real store with a mock store containing predictable test data.

This keeps your unit tests:

Fast

Reliable

Isolated from external systems

Unit testing Svelte components with Vitest is not about testing code for the sake of it. It's about **locking in correct behavior** so you can refactor, scale, and improve your applications with confidence.

By setting up a clean testing environment, writing small, focused tests for rendering and interaction, testing event dispatching properly, and mocking external dependencies when necessary, you create a strong, maintainable foundation for building real-world Svelte applications.

Testing does not slow you down. **It speeds you up** — by reducing the cost of mistakes and making good development safe.

End-to-End Testing with Playwright

Unit testing components ensures that small pieces of your application behave correctly. But applications are not just isolated components — they are full experiences, spanning multiple pages, forms, interactions, and server calls.

End-to-end (E2E) testing validates the complete behavior of your application, from a real user's perspective. It simulates how a user navigates, interacts, and expects the system to respond, using real browsers and real DOM events — not mocks.

In professional Svelte projects, **Playwright** stands out as the most reliable, developer-friendly framework for end-to-end testing. It is fast, supports multiple browsers (Chromium, Firefox, WebKit), and gives you powerful control over browser interactions.

Setting Up Playwright for a Svelte Project

Start by installing Playwright and its test runner:

```
npm install --save-dev @playwright/test

npx playwright install
```

This does two things:

Installs the Playwright framework.

Downloads browser binaries (Chromium, Firefox, WebKit) so you can test across different browsers.

Once installed, create a basic test configuration in `playwright.config.js`:

```js
// playwright.config.js
import { defineConfig } from '@playwright/test';

export default defineConfig({
    testDir: './tests',
    use: {
        baseURL: 'http://localhost:5173',
        headless: true,
        screenshot: 'only-on-failure',
        video: 'retain-on-failure',
        trace: 'on-first-retry'
    }
});
```

This setup:

Assumes your app runs locally at `localhost:5173` (default for Vite/SvelteKit).

Takes screenshots and videos only on test failures.

Enables traces to debug flaky tests easily.

Make sure your development server is running before running Playwright tests.

Writing Your First End-to-End Test

Let's write a basic test for a login flow.

Suppose you have a /login page with a form:

```
<!-- src/routes/login/+page.svelte -->
<form>
    <input placeholder="Email" />
    <input type="password" placeholder="Password"
/>
    <button type="submit">Login</button>
</form>
```

You want to test that a user can:

Navigate to /login

Enter email and password

Submit the form

Get redirected to /dashboard

See a welcome message

Create a test file:

```
mkdir tests

touch tests/login.spec.js
```

Write the test:

```
// tests/login.spec.js
import { test, expect } from '@playwright/test';

test('user can login and see dashboard', async ({
page }) => {
    await page.goto('/login');

    await page.fill('input[placeholder="Email"]',
'test@example.com');
    await
page.fill('input[placeholder="Password"]',
'password123');

    await page.click('button:has-text("Login")');
```

```
      await expect(page).toHaveURL('/dashboard');
      await
expect(page.locator('h1')).toContainText('Welcome')
;
});
```

Breaking it down:

`page.goto('/login')` navigates to the login page.

`page.fill()` types into input fields.

`page.click()` submits the form.

`expect(page).toHaveURL()` checks that the page redirected correctly.

`expect(page.locator('h1')).toContainText()` asserts that the dashboard rendered the correct heading.

To run the test:

```
npx playwright test
```

If your login flow is working, the test will pass. If anything breaks (wrong URL, wrong text), the test fails — giving you actionable feedback.

Testing Different Browsers

By default, Playwright can run tests across Chromium, Firefox, and WebKit.

You can test across all three by running:

```
npx playwright test --project=chromium

npx playwright test --project=firefox

npx playwright test --project=webkit
```

Or configure multiple projects inside `playwright.config.js`:

```
projects: [
      { name: 'chromium', use: { browserName:
'chromium' } },
```

```
      { name: 'firefox', use: { browserName:
'firefox' } },
      { name: 'webkit', use: { browserName: 'webkit'
} }
]
```

Testing across multiple browsers helps you catch issues early — like CSS inconsistencies, event handling quirks, or unsupported features.

Professional applications almost always validate behavior in at least two browsers.

Working with Authentication and Sessions

Real applications often require login before accessing pages. Testing authenticated flows requires managing sessions.

You can:

Log in programmatically using API calls

Save and reuse cookies

Use test hooks (beforeEach) to handle authentication

Example of authenticating via UI before a test:

```
test.beforeEach(async ({ page }) => {
     await page.goto('/login');
     await page.fill('input[placeholder="Email"]',
'test@example.com');
     await
page.fill('input[placeholder="Password"]',
'password123');
     await page.click('button:has-text("Login")');

     await expect(page):toHaveURL('/dashboard');
});
```

Now every test that runs after this automatically starts from a logged-in state.

For faster tests, you can also create a one-time login fixture that saves session storage or cookies and restores them before each test.

Managing Flaky Tests and Timing Issues

End-to-end tests can sometimes be flaky if you don't handle **timing** properly.

Always **wait for stable conditions** before making assertions.

For example, after submitting a form:

```
await Promise.all([

    page.waitForNavigation(),

    page.click('button:has-text("Submit")')

]);
```

or after dynamic content loads:

```
await expect(page.locator('.user-
profile')).toBeVisible();
```

Never use raw `setTimeout()` delays.
Use Playwright's built-in waiting mechanisms (like `waitForSelector`, `waitForResponse`, `expect.toBeVisible()`) — they are smarter and avoid slowing tests unnecessarily.

Handling timing well makes your E2E tests:

Fast

Reliable

Maintainable

Practical Exercise: Testing a Full Workflow

Suppose your Svelte app lets users:

Sign up

Log in

Update their profile

Log out

Your full end-to-end test might look like this:

```
test('new user signup, profile update, and logout',
async ({ page }) => {
    await page.goto('/signup');

    await page.fill('input[placeholder="Email"]',
'newuser@example.com');
    await
page.fill('input[placeholder="Password"]',
'newpassword');
    await page.click('button:has-text("Sign
Up")');

    await expect(page).toHaveURL('/dashboard');

    await page.goto('/profile');
    await page.fill('input[placeholder="Name"]',
'New User');
    await page.click('button:has-text("Save")');

    await
expect(page.locator('h1')).toContainText('Profile
updated');

    await page.click('button:has-text("Logout")');
    await expect(page).toHaveURL('/');
});
```

This one test covers multiple major workflows — signup, profile management, and logout.

With just a few lines of code, you verify end-to-end functionality that could otherwise break unnoticed in production.

End-to-end testing with Playwright is not just a bonus for large teams. It's a **core practice** for any serious Svelte project — whether you're building for 100 users or 1 million.

By writing focused, meaningful E2E tests, simulating real user behavior, managing authentication flows cleanly, and avoiding flaky patterns through smart waiting strategies, you ensure that:

Major workflows work consistently

Regressions are caught immediately

Your development and deployment pipelines stay safe and reliable

End-to-end testing doesn't slow down development — it **accelerates confidence** and **raises quality** at every level.

Debugging Reactive State and Performance Bottlenecks

As you build larger Svelte applications, there will come a point where something unexpected happens. A component doesn't update when you expect it to. Something renders multiple times unnecessarily. The app feels slower after a new feature was added.

When these problems arise, you need the right techniques to **debug reactivity issues** and **identify performance bottlenecks** efficiently — not by guessing, but by understanding exactly how your code behaves.

Understanding How Svelte's Reactivity Works

Svelte's reactivity is based on **assignment tracking**.

When you assign to a variable that is referenced in the template or a reactive statement, Svelte automatically schedules an update to the DOM.

```
<script>
    let count = 0;

    function increment() {
        count += 1; // triggers reactivity
    }
</script>

<button on:click={increment}>
    Clicked {count} times
</button>
```

If you **mutate an object or array** without assigning it again, Svelte will **not** detect a change:

```
<script>
    let items = [];

    function addItem() {
        items.push('new item'); // mutation
without assignment: no update
    }
</script>
```

To trigger an update, **you must assign**:

```
items = [...items, 'new item'];
```

This is the number one source of confusion and subtle bugs in Svelte reactivity:

Mutations alone don't trigger updates. Only assignments do.

When debugging reactive issues, your first instinct should always be to check:

Did I mutate something without reassigning?

Did I forget to create a new array or object?

Debugging Reactive State in Practice

Sometimes you aren't sure whether your reactive statements are running correctly.

Svelte provides an easy way to observe reactive updates: **logging inside $: reactive statements**.

Suppose you have:

```
<script>

    let name = '';

    let greeting;


    $: greeting = `Hello, ${name}`;

</script>
```

You can add a debug log:

```
<script>
    let name = '';
    let greeting;

    $: {
        console.log('Reactive greeting updated:',
name);
        greeting = `Hello, ${name}`;
    }
</script>
```

Now every time `name` changes, you'll see a clear console log showing when and why the reactive block re-executed.

You can do this anywhere — and it's one of the most powerful, low-friction debugging techniques for Svelte reactivity.

Using the Svelte DevTools Extension

Svelte DevTools is a browser extension that gives you a real-time view of your component tree, props, stores, and reactive values.

You can:

Inspect current values inside each component

Watch reactive assignments live

See when and why components re-render

Trace context propagation and store usage

Installing Svelte DevTools:

Chrome Web Store: "Svelte Devtools"

Firefox Add-ons: "Svelte Devtools"

Edge Add-ons: "Svelte Devtools"

Once installed:

Open DevTools (F12).

Navigate to the Svelte tab.

Inspect your app's live state.

For reactive debugging, Svelte DevTools saves an enormous amount of time — especially in large applications where manually tracking state would otherwise be tedious.

Profiling Performance with Browser Tools

Sometimes your app works correctly, but **feels slow** — components re-render more often than needed, or updates lag after user input.

To find bottlenecks, use the browser's built-in **Performance profiler**:

Open DevTools → Performance tab.

Start recording.

Interact with your application (navigate, click, load).

Stop recording.

Analyze:

Look at scripting times.

Find frames that take too long (>16ms blocks smooth 60fps rendering).

Check which components re-rendered and how often.

When inspecting the profile, focus on:

Expensive reactive blocks (loops, derived calculations)

Repeated DOM updates that could be batched

Heavy JavaScript execution triggered by simple actions

Goal: Keep the main thread work under 16 milliseconds per frame.

Real-World Example: Debugging a Slow Dashboard

Suppose your dashboard has a table that feels sluggish when you add rows dynamically.

You check your table rendering code:

```
<script>
    let items = [];

    function addRow() {
        items.push({ id: Math.random(), value:
'New row' });
    }
</script>

<button on:click={addRow}>Add Row</button>

<table>
    {#each items as item}
        <tr><td>{item.value}</td></tr>
    {/each}
</table>
```

Problem:

You mutated `items` with `.push()`, but **did not reassign it** — so Svelte does not trigger a re-render properly.

Some frames get stuck, causing layout thrashing.

Fix:

```
function addRow() {

    items = [...items, { id: Math.random(), value:
'New row' }];
}
```

By assigning a new array, you tell Svelte explicitly: **this value changed, please update.**

After this fix, you record another performance trace and notice:

No more janky frames

Smooth insertion of new rows

Reactivity now correctly updating the DOM

This small pattern — always assigning, never just mutating — fixes a huge number of performance and correctness problems.

Optimizing Expensive Derived Computations

Derived computations — like expensive `map`, `filter`, or `sort` operations — can cause unnecessary recalculations.

Suppose you have:

```
<script>

    let bigList = []; // thousands of items



    $: filteredList = bigList.filter(item =>
item.active);

</script>
```

If `bigList` rarely changes, but the component re-renders often (due to other inputs), recalculating `filteredList` every time wastes CPU cycles.

You can optimize using a **derived store** or **memoization pattern**.

Example using a derived store:

```
import { writable, derived } from 'svelte/store';



export const bigList = writable([]);



export const filteredList = derived(bigList,
($bigList) =>

    $bigList.filter(item => item.active)

);
```
In the component:

```
<script>
    import { filteredList } from
'$lib/stores/listStore.js';
</script>

{#each $filteredList as item}
    <p>{item.name}</p>
{/each}
```

Now the expensive `.filter()` only runs when `bigList` actually changes, not on every unrelated render.

This kind of careful optimization keeps your large lists and dashboards responsive even with tens of thousands of entries.

Debugging and optimizing Svelte applications is not about guessing why something feels wrong.
It's about **understanding reactivity**, **observing your application carefully**, and **using the right tools and patterns** to find and fix problems.

Chapter 8: Optimizing for High Performance

In modern web development, users expect web applications to load quickly, respond immediately, and stay smooth even under heavy load. No matter how polished your UI is or how clever your features are, **performance** defines the user's experience.

Building fast applications with Svelte isn't about guesswork. It's about **intentionally designing for performance**: minimizing the amount of code users download, reducing unnecessary work in the browser, and tuning your application based on real-world metrics — not assumptions.

Bundle Size Reduction, Code Splitting, and Tree Shaking

When building modern web applications, performance starts long before a user interacts with your UI.
It begins the moment your application starts loading.

The larger your JavaScript bundles are, the longer it takes before your users can see anything. Slow bundle downloads lead to longer **Time to First Paint (FCP)**, **Time to Interactive (TTI)**, and directly hurt user experience, especially on mobile or slower networks.

In Svelte, because of the compiler-first approach, we already have a smaller baseline compared to most frameworks. But that alone is not enough. **Intentional bundle optimization** is critical for building production-grade applications.

In this section, we'll walk through how to **reduce your bundle size, split your code smartly**, and **take advantage of tree shaking** to remove dead weight automatically — all with real-world, actionable examples.

Why Bundle Size Matters So Much

Every kilobyte you send to the user:

Increases load time

Blocks interactivity

Consumes more mobile data

Increases bounce rates

Google research shows that pages taking longer than 3 seconds to load lose **53%** of mobile users.

When your application loads faster, users stay longer, interact more, and trust your app more.

Reducing your JavaScript size isn't optional. It's a requirement for serious development.

Tree Shaking in Svelte and Vite

Tree shaking is the process of removing unused code from your final JavaScript bundles.

Svelte and Vite already perform tree shaking automatically during production builds — but it only works **if your code is structured properly**.

To fully benefit from tree shaking:

Use ES module syntax (`import/export`) consistently.

Avoid importing entire libraries if you only need one function.

Avoid dynamic require/imports unless necessary.

Practical Example: Good vs Bad Imports

Suppose you use a utility library with lots of functions:

Bad practice (prevents tree shaking):

```
import * as utils from '$lib/utils';
```

This pulls in **all** utility functions — even if you use only one.

Better practice (enables tree shaking):

```
import { formatDate } from
'$lib/utils/formatDate.js';
```

138

Now, only the `formatDate` function is included in the bundle.

Key rule: Always import **only what you need**, not everything.

This pattern alone can easily reduce your bundle size by 10%–30% in large projects.

Code Splitting: Only Loading What You Need

Code splitting breaks your JavaScript into multiple smaller files (chunks), so that:

Only the code needed for the current page or feature is loaded immediately.

The rest is loaded **on-demand** when the user navigates or interacts.

In SvelteKit, route-based code splitting is automatic:

Each `+page.svelte` generates a separate chunk.

Navigation between pages loads only the relevant chunk.

You don't have to manually configure it — just structure your routes normally.

Manually Splitting Code Inside a Page

Sometimes you have a very large component or library that you don't want to include in the initial page load.

You can manually split and lazy-load modules using dynamic imports:

Example: Loading a large chart library only when needed.

```
<script>
    let ChartComponent = null;

    async function loadChart() {
        const module = await
import('$lib/components/BigChart.svelte');
        ChartComponent = module.default;
    }
</script>

<button on:click={loadChart}>Load Chart</button>
```

```
{#if ChartComponent}
    <svelte:component this={ChartComponent} />
{/if}
```

When the user clicks "Load Chart":

Only then is the `BigChart.svelte` component downloaded.

Until then, it's not part of the initial bundle.

This approach dramatically improves your app's initial loading time, especially for pages with expensive, rarely used features like analytics panels, editors, or complex visualizations.

Real-World Example: Dashboard Optimization

Suppose you are building a dashboard with:

Core user profile panel

Heavy analytics chart using a charting library

Rich text editor for user notes

If you import everything statically, your initial bundle could balloon to **over 1MB**.

But with smart code splitting:

Profile section loads immediately (~50KB)

Analytics chart loads only when user clicks "View Analytics"

Editor loads only when user clicks "Edit Notes"

Your initial page loads 5–10× faster, because users download only what they need when they need it.

This also avoids wasting bandwidth on users who never use the heavy features.

Identifying Bundle Bloat

Sometimes, third-party libraries you add seem small but balloon your bundle unexpectedly.

Use bundle analysis tools to catch this.

Vite offers a great plugin: **rollup-plugin-visualizer**.

Install it:

```
npm install --save-dev rollup-plugin-visualizer
```

Update your `vite.config.js`:

```
import { visualizer } from 'rollup-plugin-
visualizer';

export default {
    plugins: [
        sveltekit(),
        visualizer({ open: true })
    ]
};
```

Now run:

npm run build

It will open a treemap showing:

Which files take the most space

Which dependencies are bloating your app

Which chunks are loaded eagerly vs lazily

Focus first on:

Removing unused packages

Replacing heavy libraries with lighter alternatives

Splitting large internal modules if needed

Optimizing External Libraries

Sometimes you can't remove a dependency entirely — but you can **optimize how you import it**.

Example: Icon libraries.

Bad practice:

```
import { AllIcons } from 'some-icon-library';
```

This pulls in hundreds of SVGs into your bundle.

Better practice:

```
import { HomeIcon } from 'lucide-svelte';
```

This imports only the exact icons you need.

Another example: Dates and times.

Instead of:

```
import moment from 'moment';
```

Use:

```
import { format, parseISO } from 'date-fns';
```

moment.js is over **200KB gzipped**.
date-fns functions are small, modular, and tree-shakable.

These small decisions make a massive cumulative difference.

Real Exercise: Shrinking a Bloated Bundle

Suppose you find your bundle is 800KB after a build.

Analysis reveals:

300KB is a charting library you only use on one page.

200KB is a UI library where you use only 5 out of 200 components.

100KB is moment.js for date formatting.

Optimization steps:

Lazy-load the charting component with dynamic `import()`.

Manually import only needed components from the UI library.

Replace moment.js with date-fns, importing only the specific utilities.

After optimization:

Initial bundle drops to 250KB.

First paint happens under 1 second on average mobile devices.

TTI improves significantly.

This workflow is not theoretical. It is exactly what high-performing web applications do behind the scenes to stay competitive.

Reducing bundle size through **tree shaking**, **code splitting**, and **smart dependency management** is not about micro-optimizations. It's about delivering **real, noticeable speed improvements** that users feel immediately.

Minimizing Re-Renders and Reactive Overheads

One of Svelte's most powerful features is its highly optimized reactivity system.
By compiling reactivity into direct DOM operations, Svelte avoids the virtual DOM overhead of frameworks like React.

However, this does not mean that performance is automatic. Poor reactive patterns can still cause unnecessary recalculations, extra re-renders, and sluggish behavior — especially as your application grows larger.

Professional Svelte applications require **intentional design** to minimize reactivity overhead and ensure updates are targeted, efficient, and fast.

In Svelte, **a component re-renders** whenever:

A bound variable it uses **is reassigned**.

A **store it subscribes to** emits a new value.

A **parent component passes a changed prop**.

Svelte's updates are granular — it doesn't re-render the whole tree unless necessary.
Still, if you group too much reactive state together, even small changes can cause bigger sections of the DOM to update than needed.

When debugging performance, your goal is to **limit the scope of updates** to only the elements that need it.

Reassign Instead of Mutating

A very common source of unnecessary overhead comes from direct mutations without triggering reactivity.

For example:

```
<script>
    let items = [{ id: 1, name: 'Item 1' }, { id:
2, name: 'Item 2' }];

    function addItem() {
        items.push({ id: 3, name: 'Item 3' }); //
mutation, no reactivity triggered
    }
</script>
```

The `push()` modifies `items`, but Svelte does not detect a change because **no assignment** happened.

Correct approach:

```
function addItem() {
    items = [...items, { id: 3, name: 'Item 3' }];
}
```
Assignment is what triggers Svelte's compiled update hooks.

Every time you update an array, object, or Map, **reassign** a new copy if you expect the UI to reflect it.

Structuring State for Minimal Updates

Another important strategy is to **keep reactive state small and focused**.

Suppose you have this:

```
<script>
    let dashboardState = {
        profile: { name: 'Jane', age: 30 },
        notifications: [],
        activityFeed: [],
```

```
    };
</script>
```

Whenever you update any part of `dashboardState`, all sections depending on it might re-render, even if only one small property changed.

Instead, split state logically:

```
<script>
    let profile = { name: 'Jane', age: 30 };
    let notifications = [];
    let activityFeed = [];
</script>
```

Now, updates to `notifications` won't cause `profile` or `activityFeed` to re-render.

This separation isolates updates naturally — keeping your UI efficient and predictable.

Breaking Components into Smaller Pieces

Large components that manage multiple concerns can suffer from unnecessary updates because **everything depends on everything**.

Break your interface into smaller, self-contained components.

Instead of:

```
<!-- HugeDashboard.svelte -->

<ProfileSection {profileData} />

<ActivityFeed {activityData} />

<NotificationsPanel {notifications} />
```

Each subcomponent (`ProfileSection`, `ActivityFeed`, `NotificationsPanel`) should:

Accept only the minimal props it needs.

Manage its own state where appropriate.

Update independently.

For instance, if new notifications arrive, only `NotificationsPanel` needs to re-render — not the entire dashboard.

This **component isolation** keeps your application snappy, even under constant updates.

Avoiding Over-Reactive Derived Computations

Derived reactive values are powerful but can become expensive if not handled carefully.

Suppose you have:

```
<script>
    let items = []; // thousands of items
    let search = '';

    $: filteredItems = items.filter(item =>
item.name.includes(search));
</script>
```

Every time `search` changes — such as typing a single letter — Svelte recalculates `filteredItems` across all `items`.

If the list is large, this becomes costly very quickly.

Solution: **debounce** the search input and **memoize** heavy computations.

Example:

```
<script>
    import { debounce } from
'$lib/utils/debounce.js';

    let items = [];
    let search = '';
    let debouncedSearch = '';

    const updateSearch = debounce((value) => {
        debouncedSearch = value;
    }, 300);
```

```
    $: updateSearch(search);

    $: filteredItems = items.filter(item =>
item.name.includes(debouncedSearch));
</script>
```

Now, filtering happens only after the user stops typing for 300ms — improving responsiveness dramatically.

Using $: if (...) Blocks Wisely

Reactive statements can be optimized further using conditions.

Instead of recalculating unnecessarily:

```
<script>
    let user = null;

    $: userRole = user ? user.role : 'guest';
</script>
```

You can scope reactive work more tightly:

```
<script>
    let user = null;
    let userRole = 'guest';

    $: if (user) {
        userRole = user.role;
    }
</script>
```

This avoids recomputing userRole when unrelated state changes.

The smaller and more precise your reactive statements, the faster your updates stay.

Real-World Debugging Example: Input Lag in a Search Box

Suppose users report that typing into your search box feels slow.

You check your code:

```
<script>
```

```
    let search = '';
    let users = []; // loaded elsewhere

    $: filtered = users.filter(user =>
user.name.includes(search));
</script>
```

Problem:

Every keystroke triggers a heavy `.filter()` on possibly thousands of users.

Solution:

Add a 200ms debounce on search input.

Only filter after debounce fires.

Only re-render filtered list after debounce.

New code:

```
<script>
    import { debounce } from
'$lib/utils/debounce.js';

    let search = '';
    let debouncedSearch = '';

    const updateDebouncedSearch = debounce((value)
=> {
        debouncedSearch = value;
    }, 200);

    $: updateDebouncedSearch(search);

    let users = [];

    $: filtered = users.filter(user =>
user.name.includes(debouncedSearch));
</script>
```

Result:

No more input lag.

UI stays fast and smooth even with very large user lists.

Performance in Svelte isn't just about raw speed — it's about **doing the minimal necessary work at the right time**.

By:

Reassigning instead of mutating

Structuring state finely

Splitting components smartly

Managing reactive statements precisely

Debouncing and memoizing heavy computations

you ensure your Svelte applications stay fast, efficient, and pleasant to use — even as data, features, and complexity grow.

Profiling and Performance Tuning Techniques

Building a fast Svelte application isn't about guessing where the bottlenecks are.
It's about measuring real performance, finding real issues, and fixing them precisely — based on facts, not intuition.

Performance tuning without profiling is like repairing a machine blindfolded. You might fix something, or you might break something else. In professional development, **profiling** always comes before **optimization**.

Key Principles Before Tuning Anything

Measure first, fix second.
Never optimize based on assumptions. Always verify real performance problems first.

Prioritize   **impact.**
Fix slow, frequent operations first — not rare edge cases.

Focus on user experience metrics.
Speed perceived by users matters more than synthetic benchmarks.

149

When you stick to these principles, you stop wasting time on irrelevant micro-optimizations and instead focus on meaningful improvements.

Profiling JavaScript and Rendering Performance

The first tool every Svelte developer should master is **Chrome DevTools' Performance Profiler**.

Here's the exact workflow:

Step 1: Record a Profile

Open your app in Chrome.

Open DevTools → **Performance** tab.

Click **Record**.

Perform the interactions you want to analyze — loading pages, typing into forms, clicking buttons.

Click **Stop Recording**.

You now have a complete timeline showing:

Scripting time (JavaScript execution)

Rendering time (DOM updates)

Painting time (visual updates)

Layout shifts (potential jank)

Step 2: Analyze Major Bottlenecks

In the Performance panel, look for:

Long tasks: Any single task >50ms blocks the main thread and hurts responsiveness.

Layout thrashing: Multiple forced reflows can cause frames to drop.

Large script evaluations: Loading too much JavaScript up front can block first paint.

Each event is clickable — you can inspect precisely what function or component caused the delay.

You are looking for evidence, not guesses.

Key Metrics to Pay Attention To

When profiling Svelte apps, focus on these critical user-centric metrics:

First Contentful Paint (FCP):
How quickly the first visible part of the page renders.

Time to Interactive (TTI):
How soon after loading users can interact without lag.

Long Tasks:
Tasks over 50ms that block interactivity.

Frames Per Second (FPS):
Aim to keep 60fps consistently, especially during animations or dynamic updates.

Cumulative Layout Shift (CLS):
Avoid unexpected jumps in layout as content loads.

If these metrics are healthy, your application feels fast. If any are bad, users will feel friction, even if the app "works."

Real Example: Diagnosing a Slow Dashboard

Suppose your dashboard page feels slow when switching between tabs.

You record a profile and find:

A long 120ms scripting task triggered when clicking a tab.

Inside that task, a `.filter()` operation over a 10,000-item array.

Problem: Filtering a massive dataset synchronously blocks the main thread.

Solution:

Virtualize the list so only visible items are rendered (e.g., with **svelte-virtual**).

Move expensive filtering operations into Web Workers if needed.

Use debounced user inputs to limit recalculations.

Result:

Tab switch feels instant.

Main thread is freed to handle user input quickly.

Frame times drop below 16ms again, restoring 60fps.

This is performance tuning based on real profiling, not guesswork.

Bundle Size and Loading Performance Profiling

Frontend performance isn't just about execution time. **Bundle size directly impacts loading time**.

Large bundles mean:

Slower download

Slower parsing

Slower first paint

Worse TTI

Step 1: Measure Bundle Size

Use `vite build --analyze` or install `rollup-plugin-visualizer` to generate a treemap showing:

How big each dependency is

How much each route costs

Where unexpected bloat comes from

If you find:

Huge UI libraries (like importing all of Material UI)

Full charting libraries on pages that don't need them

Moment.js instead of date-fns

Then you have identified **optimization targets**.

Step 2: Fix Heavy Dependencies

You can:

Replace heavy libraries with lighter alternatives.

Import only what you need (named imports, not wildcards).

Lazy-load large features using dynamic `import()` only when necessary.

Example: Shrinking a Dashboard Bundle

Before optimization:

Initial dashboard bundle: 1.2MB.

Largest chunk: Full chart.js library, even on pages not using charts.

After optimization:

Code-split chart features behind a "View Analytics" button.

Bundle drops to 400KB for initial load.

First paint happens under 1 second.

This drastically improves both perceived and measured speed — and was entirely based on profiling data.

Monitoring Runtime Reactivity

Svelte's reactivity system is fast, but heavy use of reactive statements, large computed lists, or frequent updates can still create runtime bottlenecks.

When performance feels wrong but you don't see major scripting tasks, inspect your reactive flow:

Are reactive computations too broad? (`$: hugeList.map(...)`)

Are reactive statements triggering too often?

Are components re-rendering unnecessarily because of prop changes?

Use **Svelte DevTools** to:

Watch when components re-render.

Inspect stores and reactive values.

Find unexpected state changes.

Example: If typing into a small form causes unrelated components to re-render, it's a clear sign that state is too broadly scoped.

Fix: Localize reactive state or break up components more cleanly.

Practical Exercise: End-to-End Profiling

Let's walk through a full profiling exercise for a real feature:

Suppose you add a "Search Products" feature on an ecommerce site.

Record performance:

Notice input feels laggy after a few letters.

Inspect scripting tasks:

Long tasks caused by recalculating a full 5,000-item product list on every keystroke.

Analyze reactivity:

Reactive statement recalculates `.filter()` immediately on every letter.

Apply fixes:

Debounce search input with a 300ms delay.

Move filtering to a derived store.

Only display 20 results per page (pagination).

Re-profile:

No more long tasks.

Input feels instant.

Frame rate remains stable.

This is how professional performance tuning works: **Measure → Identify → Fix → Validate**.

Performance tuning isn't about clever tricks. It's about systematically **profiling real user interactions**, **identifying bottlenecks**, and **applying targeted optimizations** that make a measurable difference.

By:

Measuring JavaScript execution

Analyzing bundle sizes and loading behavior

Tracking reactivity and re-renders

Fixing issues based on real evidence

you build Svelte applications that feel lightning-fast, polished, and production-ready.

With this, you now have the full professional performance toolkit for building serious, scalable Svelte applications.

Chapter 9: Accessibility, Internationalization, and UX at Scale

When building small prototypes, it's easy to focus purely on functionality — whether the button works, whether the data loads, whether the animations play smoothly.

But when building **serious, production-grade applications**, you must address something bigger: **making your application usable by everyone, everywhere**.

Fast-loading, beautiful interfaces mean nothing if users can't access them, can't read them, or can't interact with them because of physical, language, or cognitive barriers.

Building Accessible and Inclusive Web Interfaces

Accessibility is not a nice-to-have.
It's a **fundamental responsibility** when building modern web applications.

When your application is accessible, you're not just ticking a compliance box. You're enabling real users — users with vision impairments, users who rely on keyboards instead of mice, users with cognitive or motor disabilities, users navigating temporary or situational challenges — to interact with your content fully and meaningfully.

In Svelte, building accessible interfaces is about **making the right choices from the start**, not patching things later. Accessibility must be baked directly into your components, layouts, navigation, and interaction patterns.

Using Semantic HTML Properly

The first and most important step in accessibility is to use the **right HTML elements for the right jobs**.

Svelte makes it easy because you write plain HTML directly. But it's still up to you to **choose correctly**.

When you need a button, use `<button>`, not a styled `<div>`. When you link somewhere, use `<a href="">`, not a `<span>` with a click event.

Example: Wrong approach

```
<div on:click={submitForm}>

    Submit

</div>
```

This looks like a button visually, but:

It's not focusable by keyboard.

It has no role for assistive devices.

Screen readers won't recognize it as actionable.

Correct approach:

```
<button on:click={submitForm}>

    Submit

</button>
```

The `<button>`:

Can be focused with Tab.

Can be clicked with Enter or Space.

Announces itself correctly to screen readers.

Behaves properly across browsers and devices.

When you use semantic elements properly, you inherit **built-in accessibility** without extra effort.

Ensuring Keyboard Navigability

Every interactive feature — navigation menus, forms, modals, buttons — must be fully operable **using only a keyboard**.

Users who cannot use a mouse, whether permanently or temporarily, rely entirely on:

Tab (move forward)

Shift+Tab (move backward)

Enter (activate buttons or links)

Space (activate buttons)

Arrow keys (navigate within widgets)

Your Svelte application must honor this model naturally.

Example: Accessible navigation menu

```svelte
<script>
    let isOpen = false;

    function toggleMenu() {
        isOpen = !isOpen;
    }
</script>

<button
    aria-expanded={isOpen}
    aria-controls="main-menu"
    on:click={toggleMenu}
>
    Menu
</button>

{#if isOpen}
    <nav id="main-menu">
        <ul>
            <li><a href="/home">Home</a></li>
            <li><a href="/about">About</a></li>
            <li><a
href="/contact">Contact</a></li>
        </ul>
```

```
        </nav>
{/if}
```

In this example:

The button controls the visibility of the menu.

`aria-expanded` tells screen readers whether the menu is open.

Navigation links inside are reachable and actionable with the keyboard.

Notice that we didn't need special JavaScript for focus management — because we used native elements properly.

If you build your application this way, keyboard users experience the same rich interactivity as mouse users.

Managing Focus and Focus States

When users navigate with a keyboard, **visible focus** is essential.

By default, browsers apply outlines to focused elements. Never disable outlines without providing a visible replacement.

Good CSS:

```
button:focus,

a:focus {

    outline: 2px solid #005fcc;

    outline-offset: 2px;

}
```

This ensures that users always know **where their focus is**.

If your design system removes outlines by default (many do), **restore them intentionally** in your components.

Also, when using modals, dialogs, or dynamic overlays, manage focus properly:

Focus should move inside the modal when it opens.

Focus should trap inside the modal while it's open.

Focus should return to the triggering element when the modal closes.

Svelte doesn't do this automatically — but it's easy to handle using lifecycle hooks.

Example: Basic focus trap setup

```
<script>
    import { onMount } from 'svelte';

    let modalRef;

    onMount(() => {
        modalRef.focus();
    });
</script>

<div
    tabindex="0"
    bind:this={modalRef}
    role="dialog"
    aria-modal="true"
>
    <h2>Modal Title</h2>
    <p>Modal content here...</p>
    <button on:click={closeModal}>Close</button>
</div>
```

Setting `tabindex="0"` and focusing the container ensures that screen readers and keyboard users are anchored immediately into the modal context.

For production apps, consider using a small focus-trap library if your dialogs become complex.

Providing Meaningful Text Alternatives

Screen readers do not "see" images, icons, or decorative UI. They need **textual descriptions** to interpret visual information.

Key rules:

Every meaningful image must have an `alt` attribute.

Every icon that conveys information must have a text alternative.

Decorative images should have `alt=""` so they are skipped.

Examples:

Correct descriptive image:

```
<img src="/user-avatar.jpg" alt="Profile photo of
John Doe" />
```

Correct decorative image:

```
<img src="/divider-line.svg" alt="" aria-
hidden="true" />
```

Correct icon button:

```
<button aria-label="Close notification"
on:click={closeNotification}>

     <svg>...</svg>

</button>
```

If your SVG conveys action or meaning, and you don't provide an `aria-label`, screen reader users may have no idea what the button does.

Providing correct alternatives ensures that all users — visual and non-visual — understand what is happening.

Using ARIA Roles and Properties Appropriately

ARIA (Accessible Rich Internet Applications) helps when you create custom interactive patterns that native HTML cannot fully express.

Use ARIA carefully and only when necessary.

Common helpful ARIA attributes:

`aria-expanded` for toggled states

`aria-controls` for controlled regions

`aria-label` for unlabeled buttons or inputs

`aria-hidden` for purely decorative elements

Example: Accordion component

```
<script>
    let expanded = false;
</script>

<button
    aria-expanded={expanded}
    aria-controls="accordion-content"
    on:click={() => expanded = !expanded}
>
    Show Details
</button>

{#if expanded}
    <div id="accordion-content">
        <p>Extra information here...</p>
    </div>
{/if}
```

Here:

`aria-expanded` dynamically reflects open/closed state.

`aria-controls` connects the button to the collapsible content.

This pattern makes your accordion fully understandable to assistive technologies.

Never invent new ARIA roles unless you fully understand what you're doing. Stick with established, documented roles unless absolutely necessary.

Real-World Example: Making a Data Table Accessible

Suppose you're building a data table of users.

Without accessibility:

```
<table>

    <tr><td>John Doe</td><td>Admin</td></tr>
```

```
    <tr><td>Jane Smith</td><td>Editor</td></tr>
</table>
```

This looks fine visually but lacks context.

Accessible version:

```
<table>
    <thead>
        <tr>
            <th scope="col">Name</th>
            <th scope="col">Role</th>
        </tr>
    </thead>
    <tbody>
        <tr>
            <td>John Doe</td>
            <td>Admin</td>
        </tr>
        <tr>
            <td>Jane Smith</td>
            <td>Editor</td>
        </tr>
    </tbody>
</table>
```

Using `<thead>`, `<tbody>`, and `<th scope="col">` gives screen readers the structure they need:

Identifying column headers

Reading tables row-by-row clearly

Maintaining orientation inside larger tables

Proper table markup is simple but incredibly powerful for accessibility.

Accessibility is not an afterthought.
It is **professional engineering practice**.

By:

Writing semantic HTML first

Ensuring full keyboard support

Managing focus intentionally

Providing meaningful text alternatives

Using ARIA roles and properties appropriately

you create Svelte applications that serve every user equally — not just users who can see, click, and move exactly the way you expect.

When you design inclusively from the beginning, your applications become better for everyone — faster, clearer, easier to use, and more humane.

Internationalization (i18n) Strategies with Svelte

Building for the web means building for a global audience. Even if your initial users are mostly local, scaling any real product requires you to **prepare your application to speak multiple languages**, adapt to different date and number formats, and respect diverse cultural norms.

Internationalization — often abbreviated as **i18n** — is the process of designing and structuring your application so that it can be **translated and localized** without needing major code changes.

In Svelte, there's no built-in internationalization system.
That's an advantage, not a weakness.
It means you have full control to implement i18n **in a way that fits your project's needs cleanly and efficiently**.

Setting Up a Simple and Scalable i18n Framework

The foundation of internationalization is separating **text** from **code**.

Hardcoding text directly into components is fine for prototypes. But for real applications, every visible string should be managed externally, in a structure that can be translated easily.

Step 1: Define Your Translation Dictionaries

Organize translations by language.

Example for English (`en.js`):

```
// src/lib/i18n/en.js
export default {
    common: {
        ok: "OK",
        cancel: "Cancel",
    },
    login: {
        title: "Login",
        username: "Username",
        password: "Password",
        submit: "Sign In"
    }
};
```

Example for Spanish (es.js):

```
// src/lib/i18n/es.js
export default {
    common: {
        ok: "Aceptar",
        cancel: "Cancelar",
    },
    login: {
        title: "Iniciar sesión",
        username: "Nombre de usuario",
        password: "Contraseña",
        submit: "Entrar"
    }
};
```

By structuring translations logically (grouped by page, feature, or component), you make it easy to maintain them as the app grows.

Step 2: Create a Translation Store

Now set up a Svelte store to manage the current language and active dictionary.

```
// src/lib/i18n/i18n.js
import { writable, derived } from 'svelte/store';
import en from './en.js';
import es from './es.js';
```

```
const dictionaries = { en, es };

export const language = writable('en');

export const dictionary = derived(language,
($language) => {
    return dictionaries[$language] ||
dictionaries.en;
});
```

This gives you:

A reactive `language` store you can update.

A reactive `dictionary` store that contains the currently active translations.

Using the Translation System Inside Components

Now you can easily use translations inside your components.

Example usage:

```
<script>
    import { dictionary } from
'$lib/i18n/i18n.js';
</script>

<h1>{$dictionary.login.title}</h1>
<form>
    <input
placeholder="{$dictionary.login.username}" />
    <input type="password"
placeholder="{$dictionary.login.password}" />
    <button type="submit">
        {$dictionary.login.submit}
    </button>
</form>
```

Whenever `language` changes, `dictionary` updates automatically, and the component re-renders with the new text.

No manual re-mounting. No messy global variables. Just simple, clean, reactive translations — the Svelte way.

Switching Languages Dynamically

You can provide users with a simple language switcher.

Example:

```
<script>
    import { language } from '$lib/i18n/i18n.js';

    function switchTo(lang) {
        language.set(lang);
    }
</script>

<button on:click={() =>
switchTo('en')}>English</button>
<button on:click={() =>
switchTo('es')}>Español</button>
```

When users click a button:

`language.set()` updates the active language.

The `dictionary` store automatically recalculates.

The UI automatically reflects the new translations.

There's no need to reload the page.
No need to reset the app.
It works reactively and instantly.

Handling Plurals and Dynamic Values

Real-world language is messy.
You can't always just substitute static text.
You need to handle plurals, variables, dates, times, and currencies.

Handling Dynamic Interpolation

You can store placeholders in your translation entries:

```
// en.js
export default {
    cart: {
```

```
          items: "{count} items in your cart"
     }
};
```

In your Svelte component:

```
<script>
     import { dictionary } from
'$lib/i18n/i18n.js';
     let itemCount = 3;
</script>


<p>{$dictionary.cart.items.replace('{count}',
itemCount)}</p>
```

This simple .replace() handles basic variable injection.

For more complex replacements (e.g., multiple placeholders), you can write a small helper function.

Example helper:

```
export function translate(template, vars) {
     return template.replace(/{(.*?)}/g, (_, key)
=> vars[key] ?? '');
}
```

Usage:

```
<script>
     import { dictionary } from
'$lib/i18n/i18n.js';
     import { translate } from
'$lib/i18n/utils.js';

     let itemCount = 3;
</script>

<p>{translate($dictionary.cart.items, { count:
itemCount })}</p>
```

Now you can inject multiple variables cleanly.

Localizing Dates, Numbers, and Currencies

Internationalization isn't just about words — it's about formats.

Different regions represent dates, numbers, and money differently.

You should never hardcode formatting logic.
Use the browser's built-in **Intl** **APIs**, which handle localization automatically.

Date Formatting

```
<script>
    let today = new Date();
</script>

<p>{new Intl.DateTimeFormat('en-
US').format(today)}</p>
<p>{new Intl.DateTimeFormat('es-
ES').format(today)}</p>
```

In the U.S., today might be displayed as `4/28/2025`. In Spain, it would be `28/4/2025`.

You can also specify options:

```
new Intl.DateTimeFormat('fr-FR', {
    weekday: 'long',
    year: 'numeric',
    month: 'long',
    day: 'numeric'
}).format(today);
```

Result: `lundi 28 avril 2025`

Currency Formatting

```
new Intl.NumberFormat('en-US', { style: 'currency',
currency: 'USD' }).format(1234.5);
// $1,234.50

new Intl.NumberFormat('de-DE', { style: 'currency',
currency: 'EUR' }).format(1234.5);
// 1.234,50 €
```

169

Use `Intl.NumberFormat` to ensure money, prices, and counts are culturally appropriate.

Real-World Example: Dynamic Language Selection with Persistence

Suppose you want users to choose a language, and you want their choice to persist across sessions.

Enhance your `i18n.js` like this:

```
const savedLang = localStorage.getItem('lang') ||
'en';

export const language = writable(savedLang);

language.subscribe((value) => {
    localStorage.setItem('lang', value);
});
```

Now:

When users pick a language, it saves to `localStorage`.

When they reload your app, their preference is remembered automatically.

It's a small addition — but it makes your application feel respectful, polished, and truly user-centered.

Internationalization in Svelte is not complicated — if you design for it from the start.

By:

Separating text into dictionaries

Using reactive translation stores

Handling dynamic values and formatting properly

Respecting dates, numbers, and currency formats

Persisting user language preferences

you make your applications ready to grow globally — cleanly, efficiently, and professionally.

In the next section, we'll work through **Crafting Seamless User Experiences for Global Audiences**, where you'll learn how cultural nuances, layout flexibility, and performance tuning intersect with internationalization to build truly world-class applications.

Crafting Seamless User Experiences for Global Audiences

Internationalization is not just about translating text or formatting dates correctly.
It's about understanding that users from different cultures, languages, and regions interact with applications **differently**, have **different expectations**, and face **different challenges**.

When you build applications for a global audience, you must design experiences that are not just translated, but **naturally intuitive** to every user, regardless of where they come from or what device they use.

Designing Layouts that Adapt to Text Expansion

In many languages, **translations are longer** than the original English source.

For example:

English: "Login" → Spanish: "Iniciar sesión"

English: "Submit" → German: "Absenden"

On average, translated strings expand by **30–50%** compared to English.

If your UI is tightly constrained — fixed button widths, hard-coded card sizes, narrow navigation bars — your design will **break** badly when text grows.

Correct practice: **Design flexible layouts that allow natural expansion**.

For example, never do this:

```
<style>
    button {
        width: 100px;
```

```
    }
</style>

<button>Submit</button>
```

This fixed width will cause overflow or cut-off text when translated.

Instead, allow dynamic sizing:

```
<style>
    button {
        padding: 0.5rem 1rem;
        min-width: 100px;
    }
</style>

<button>Submit</button>
```

Here:

Minimum width ensures reasonable sizing initially.

Padding maintains visual balance.

Text can grow naturally without breaking layout.

Building flexibility into your layouts early saves you from major redesigns when adding new languages later.

Respecting Reading Direction (LTR and RTL)

Most Western languages (English, Spanish, French, German) are read left-to-right (LTR).

But some languages, like Arabic, Hebrew, and Persian, are read right-to-left (RTL).

If you want true global reach, your application must **mirror layouts automatically** based on reading direction.

Handling RTL properly involves:

Switching text alignment.

Flipping UI components (e.g., sidebars move from left to right).

Mirroring icons (e.g., arrows, chevrons).

You can control this with the `dir` attribute on the root element.

Example:

```
<html lang="ar" dir="rtl">
```

Then in your CSS:

```
html[dir="rtl"] {
    direction: rtl;
    text-align: right;
}

html[dir="rtl"] nav {
    flex-direction: row-reverse;
}
```

If you're using SvelteKit, you can dynamically update the `lang` and `dir` attributes at runtime when switching languages.

Always test your designs in both LTR and RTL directions to ensure nothing looks broken or confusing.

Adapting Inputs and Forms for Global Users

Forms are a major point of friction if not designed thoughtfully for global users.

Key considerations:

Name Fields

Not all cultures follow the Western "first name" and "last name" structure. Some cultures use multiple family names, or single names only.

Instead of rigidly splitting names, allow flexible name fields when appropriate.

Phone Numbers

International phone numbers vary hugely:

Different country codes

Different lengths

Different formatting conventions

Use an international phone input where users can select their country code easily.

Example:

Default value: `+1`

User can change to `+234` (Nigeria) or `+49` (Germany)

There are lightweight Svelte components like `svelte-international-phone` to help with this.

Addresses

Address formats differ by country:

Some countries put postal code first.

Some countries have province/state fields, others don't.

Do not hardcode "State" and "Zip Code" fields assuming U.S. formats. Allow flexible address structures based on country selection.

If you're using third-party address libraries, make sure they support global standards like Universal Postal Union templates.

Handling Time Zones and Regional Dates

Showing timestamps like "2025-04-28 14:00" is confusing for global users. What timezone is that? Is it UTC? Local?

When displaying times:

Always clarify the time zone (`UTC`, `GMT+1`, `PST`, etc.).

Prefer showing times in **the user's local time zone** when possible.

You can automatically detect the user's local time zone with JavaScript:

```
Intl.DateTimeFormat().resolvedOptions().timeZone
```

Then format dates appropriately:

```
new Intl.DateTimeFormat('en-US', {

    timeZone: 'America/Los_Angeles',

    dateStyle: 'medium',

    timeStyle: 'short'

}).format(new Date());
```

In Svelte, you can expose a timezone-aware date component that adapts dynamically based on detected or user-selected time zones.

When scheduling events, always allow users to see both **their local time** and the **event's original time zone** to avoid confusion.

Respecting Cultural Symbols and Colors

Design choices like icons, colors, and symbols can carry **different meanings** across cultures.

Examples:

The color white symbolizes purity in the West, but mourning in some Asian cultures.

A thumbs-up emoji is positive in many countries but offensive in others.

Icons like mailboxes, currency signs, or vehicles may look unfamiliar in different countries.

When possible:

Use **universal icons** that are globally recognizable.

Use **neutral color palettes** that adapt to cultural context.

Avoid culturally loaded symbols unless you're certain of their reception.

If you heavily localize into specific markets, consider using region-specific branding, imagery, and marketing material — but keep the core functionality consistent.

Testing Global User Experiences Properly

You cannot validate global UX with local-only testing.

At a minimum:

Test in different languages (longer text, different scripts like Arabic, Chinese, Hindi).

Test in both LTR and RTL directions.

Test with VPNs or emulators for different locations and slow networks.

Test form behaviors (names, addresses, phones) across regions.

If possible, recruit testers who are native speakers or residents in target regions.
They will catch issues that automated tools or domestic testers might miss — awkward translations, confusing workflows, unexpected usability challenges.

Global readiness is **proven in testing**, not just in theory.

Building seamless experiences for global users means far more than replacing English with another language.
It means **designing flexibility into your layouts, respecting cultural nuances, handling inputs thoughtfully, formatting data clearly**, and **testing across real-world scenarios**.

By:

Designing layouts that flex naturally with translation

Supporting right-to-left languages properly

Adapting forms for real-world diversity

Handling time zones, currencies, and dates globally

Being culturally sensitive and globally aware

Testing with real users across regions

you create Svelte applications that are **not just technically global**, but **genuinely welcoming, intuitive, and successful** across the world.

Chapter 10: Future-Proofing Your Svelte Applications

The only constant in software development is change. Frameworks evolve. Best practices shift. New patterns emerge. If you want your Svelte applications to remain fast, maintainable, and competitive over time, you need to **future-proof** your codebases — deliberately, carefully, and intelligently.

Future-proofing is not about chasing every trend. It's about making decisions today that ensure your projects stay **easy to update**, **easy to scale**, and **easy to adapt** as the Svelte ecosystem and web standards grow.

Preparing for Svelte 5 and Emerging Patterns

Svelte has always been unique among frontend frameworks because it compiles your components into highly efficient JavaScript at build time. Unlike frameworks that manage reactivity during runtime through a virtual DOM, Svelte shifts that work to the compiler, leading to smaller bundles, faster updates, and a simpler mental model.

However, even a well-designed system can be refined further as real-world usage uncovers patterns and pain points. Svelte 5 introduces some significant enhancements aimed at making reactivity even clearer, more explicit, and more scalable, particularly through a new concept called **runes** and improvements in **fine-grained reactivity**.

Preparing your applications today to align naturally with these evolving patterns ensures that when you are ready to upgrade, the process will be straightforward and low-risk.

In current Svelte versions, reactivity is largely based on **assignments** and **reactive declarations**.
For example, when you assign a new value to a variable, Svelte automatically schedules the DOM to update any part of the template that references that variable.

When you want to derive one value from another reactively, you use a special syntax with the `$:` label.

```
<script>
    let count = 0;

    $: doubled = count * 2;
</script>
```

Here, `doubled` automatically recalculates whenever `count` changes, and any part of the template that uses `doubled` updates accordingly.

While this system works well for many applications, it has some limitations as complexity grows. In particular, tracking dependencies through implicit assignments and reactive labels can sometimes create surprises. For instance, deeply nested dependencies, subtle circular references, or silent missed updates in very large components can be difficult to debug and optimize.

To address this, Svelte 5 introduces a new reactivity system based on **runes**.

Runes are a way of making reactivity **explicit** and **fine-grained** at the syntax level.
Instead of relying on labels and inference, you use reactive primitives — small functions — to declare reactive state and relationships directly.

A basic example in Svelte 5 using runes would look like this:

```
<script>
    import { signal } from 'svelte';

    const count = signal(0);

    const doubled = () => count() * 2;
</script>
```

Here, `signal(0)` creates a **reactive signal** holding the value 0.
Accessing `count()` reads the current value.
Setting a new value would involve calling `count.set(newValue)`.

The function `doubled` derives from `count()` reactively.
Whenever `count` changes, anything depending on `doubled()` updates automatically.

This model has several important benefits.

First, the dependencies between reactive values are completely **explicit**.
You can see at a glance that `doubled` depends only on `count`, and no hidden reactive tracking is involved.
This makes reasoning about complex applications easier and more reliable.

Second, **fine-grained reactivity** becomes possible.
Instead of updating a whole component when any reactive value changes, Svelte 5 updates **only the exact expressions and parts of the DOM** that depend on the changed signal.
This minimizes unnecessary work, especially in components with many reactive parts.

Third, signals and runes fit naturally into modern JavaScript practices like composability and separation of concerns.
Since reactive values are ordinary functions and objects, you can pass them around, compose them into derived signals, or integrate them into utility modules without needing special compiler tricks.

It is important to recognize that Svelte 5 will not break existing Svelte 3 or 4 projects.
The $: reactive syntax will continue to be supported during the transition.
However, adopting some habits now will make future migration easier and more natural.

One habit is **isolating derived values** more cleanly.
Instead of scattering reactive statements across multiple unrelated variables, keep related reactive values together, as if they were organized functions.

Another habit is **minimizing deeply nested reactivity**.
If you have a chain where variable A depends on B, which depends on C, which depends on D, consider whether you can flatten or restructure those dependencies more cleanly.

You can also begin thinking of your state in terms of **read functions** rather than plain variables.
Whenever you reference a reactive value, treat it conceptually as something you query actively rather than something you passively expect to stay synchronized.

For stores, Svelte 5's reactivity system integrates naturally.
Writable, readable, and derived stores remain important tools, especially for shared and global state.
You can prepare by ensuring your store usage is modular, localized, and clean, avoiding tightly coupled global stores that will be harder to adapt later.

As for syntax, Svelte 5's goal with runes is to move toward a style of code where **you can immediately recognize what is reactive and what is not** without relying on compiler inference.

Instead of remembering that $: means "this code is reactive," your signals and their function calls make it obvious which parts of your code are dynamic.

Over time, this shift will help Svelte applications scale better, especially in projects with hundreds or thousands of components.

For smaller projects, the impact will be modest but still beneficial: faster updates, clearer debugging, and a more predictable programming model.

There is no urgent need to rewrite current applications today. However, designing your current and future Svelte code with **explicit, localized, modular reactivity** in mind ensures that upgrading to Svelte 5 later will be smooth and beneficial rather than stressful.

Understanding signals, explicit reactivity, and modular reactive design patterns now prepares you not only for Svelte 5 but also for broader changes happening across the web platform as reactivity becomes a more universal concept in frontend development.

When you structure your Svelte applications thoughtfully today, you are not just keeping pace — you are setting yourself up for continued success and leadership as the ecosystem evolves.

Evolving Your Architecture for Long-Term Maintainability

Building an application that works today is only part of the job. Building an application that remains understandable, adaptable, and reliable six months, one year, or three years from now is what defines a true professional approach to software development.

In Svelte projects, where it's easy to get started quickly and create impressive features in a few lines of code, it becomes even more important to **think carefully about architectural decisions** early on. Poor structure might not slow you down at the beginning, but it always becomes a burden as your codebase grows, your team expands, and new requirements emerge.

One of the most fundamental principles in long-term maintainability is **modularity**.
Modularity means building small, self-contained pieces that each do one thing well and interact with each other through clear, simple interfaces.

In a Svelte project, this starts with components. Each component should be responsible for a single clear concept. If a component grows too large or starts mixing unrelated concerns — such as handling authentication logic and rendering unrelated UI elements — it should be split into smaller components.

For example, instead of a `UserDashboard.svelte` component that handles rendering user stats, fetching notifications, managing authentication checks, and formatting dates, you would have separate components like `UserStats.svelte`, `NotificationList.svelte`, and `UserSessionManager.svelte`.

This separation makes it easy to update, test, and debug each piece independently.
If a new requirement comes in, such as changing how notifications are fetched, you can work inside `NotificationList.svelte` without touching unrelated parts of the system.

Keeping components focused also simplifies styling. Instead of one large CSS file or massive scoped styles inside a giant component, each component owns its small, specific styles. This naturally limits side effects and avoids the kind of fragile CSS that breaks unexpectedly when unrelated changes are made.

Another critical aspect of evolving maintainable architecture is **organizing your project by feature rather than by technical type**.

A common beginner mistake is creating folders like `components/`, `stores/`, and `services/`, dumping all components into one folder, all stores into another, and so on. While this looks organized initially, it quickly becomes difficult to understand how different pieces relate when your project grows past a few dozen files.

Instead, it's more scalable to organize by feature domain.

A better structure might look like this:

```
src/
  features/
    authentication/
      LoginForm.svelte
      loginStore.js
      authService.js
    dashboard/
      DashboardPage.svelte
      statsStore.js
      charts.js
    notifications/
      NotificationList.svelte
      notificationStore.js
      notificationService.js
```

Here, everything related to a particular feature — its components, stores, utilities, services — lives together in one place. When working on or debugging a feature, a developer can stay focused inside its folder, without needing to jump across different parts of the project.

This structure also scales naturally to larger teams, where different developers or squads might own different features.

It becomes easier to delegate ownership cleanly and avoid stepping on each other's work.

Maintaining a clean and scalable architecture also means **being deliberate with state management**.

State should always live at the **lowest possible level** where it still serves all the components that need it.

For instance, if a piece of state like a search query is only relevant to one small section of the page, it should be local to that component — not promoted unnecessarily to a global store.

If several sibling components need to share state, you can lift that state up to their common parent and pass it down through props. If truly global state is needed — such as user authentication status, current language, or theme settings — then a store makes sense.

In Svelte, `writable`, `readable`, and `derived` stores give you clean and simple mechanisms for managing shared state without introducing unnecessary complexity.

For example, creating a simple store for user authentication:

```
// src/features/authentication/authStore.js
import { writable } from 'svelte/store';

export const user = writable(null);

export function login(userData) {
    user.set(userData);
}

export function logout() {
    user.set(null);
}
```

Then inside any component:

```
<script>
    import { user, logout } from
'$features/authentication/authStore.js';
</script>
```

```
{#if $user}
    <p>Welcome, {$user.name}</p>
    <button on:click={logout}>Logout</button>
{:else}
    <p>Please log in</p>
{/if}
```

By structuring stores feature-by-feature like this, you avoid building one giant store that entangles unrelated concerns, which quickly becomes a source of bugs and technical debt.

Another important consideration is **future-proofing your components and stores for scalability** by using **interfaces that are easy to extend**.

Instead of designing a store around exactly what you need today, design it around concepts that are likely to evolve.

For instance, when storing user session information, don't just store `username` and `isLoggedIn` separately in different places.
Design a clean `user` object that can be easily extended if tomorrow you also need `email`, `roles`, `preferences`, or `accountStatus`.

Even if the extra fields are empty at first, your structure remains predictable and grows gracefully as features expand.

Clear naming conventions also play a massive role in long-term maintainability.

Name components, stores, and services based on what they do, not how they look or when they were created.

Names like `SidebarWidget2.svelte` or `miscStore.js` lead to confusion and slow down everyone working on the code.
Names like `NotificationList.svelte`, `UserPreferencesStore.js`, or `AuthService.js` tell you exactly what to expect without needing to read the file first.

Consistency in naming, file structure, and coding patterns across the entire project reduces cognitive load dramatically, especially as the team grows or contributors change.

Finally, maintainability depends heavily on **clear boundaries between concerns**.

Avoid mixing data fetching, formatting, and UI rendering logic inside the same component whenever possible.

Fetching data should happen through services. State management should happen through stores. Presentation logic should live inside UI components.

For example, a service for fetching notifications:

```
//
src/features/notifications/notificationService.js
export async function fetchNotifications() {
    const response = await
fetch('/api/notifications');
    if (!response.ok) {
        throw new Error('Failed to load
notifications');
    }
    return response.json();
}
```

A store managing notification data:

```
// src/features/notifications/notificationStore.js
import { writable } from 'svelte/store';
import { fetchNotifications } from
'./notificationService.js';

export const notifications = writable([]);

export async function loadNotifications() {
    const data = await fetchNotifications();
    notifications.set(data);
}
```

And then the UI stays clean and focused:

```
<script>
```

```
    import { notifications, loadNotifications }
from
'$features/notifications/notificationStore.js';

    onMount(() => {
        loadNotifications();
    });
</script>

<ul>
    {#each $notifications as notification}
        <li>{notification.message}</li>
    {/each}
</ul>
```

This clear separation means each part of your system is easier to test, debug, extend, and refactor independently.

Evolving your architecture for long-term maintainability in Svelte means **choosing clarity over cleverness**, **choosing separation over shortcuts**, and **choosing modularity over monoliths**.

By structuring components cleanly, organizing by feature, managing state deliberately, using clear interfaces, maintaining consistent naming, and separating concerns intelligently, you build applications that don't just work today — they continue to grow, adapt, and succeed over time.

Real-World Case Studies and Lessons Learned

Architectural principles are only useful when they survive the pressures of real-world applications — expanding features, growing teams, shifting requirements, tight deadlines, and unexpected challenges.

Theory alone cannot fully prepare you for how Svelte projects behave under real scaling demands.
Learning from real-world case studies — both successes and failures — gives you a deeper, grounded understanding of what it truly means to build maintainable, scalable Svelte applications.

In this section, we'll walk through real experiences drawn from production applications built with Svelte, explaining the practical architectural decisions made, the outcomes achieved, and the lessons developers learned that you can apply directly to your own work.

A mid-sized software company built an internal admin dashboard using Svelte 3 shortly after it launched.
The team had four developers and needed a fast way to replace a legacy Vue.js system that had grown sluggish and hard to maintain.

They kept their component structure modular from the beginning. Each feature — users, payments, reporting, notifications — lived in its own folder, with local components, stores, and services grouped together logically. Instead of sharing one giant global store, they created small, feature-specific stores, only promoting state to global scope when multiple features genuinely needed to observe it.

As the dashboard grew to serve over 50 internal tools, the team found that onboarding new developers remained straightforward.
New contributors could easily locate the files related to the feature they were working on, understand local data flow, and safely make changes without fear of unintended side effects elsewhere in the app.

When they decided to migrate the dashboard to SvelteKit later, they encountered very few problems.
Their modular approach meant routes, layouts, and page components could be adapted incrementally without touching unrelated parts of the system. Moving to newer reactivity patterns like more explicit derived stores was a matter of refining individual features, not rewriting the entire app.

The biggest lesson from this success was that **starting modularly** even when a project is small dramatically reduces migration costs, scaling challenges, and technical debt later.
Even when project timelines feel tight, taking the time to organize code by feature, isolate responsibilities cleanly, and minimize unnecessary coupling saves far more time and pain in the long term.

A different team building a customer-facing e-commerce site learned a harder lesson.

They initially structured their Svelte project around UI types — a `components/` folder, a `pages/` folder, a `stores/` folder — and placed global state for user sessions, cart contents, and preferences all inside a single `appStore.js` file.

As the store grew larger, different developers added new concerns into it: inventory data, marketing banners, payment status, and order history. Because every component subscribed to the same store, unrelated UI elements began updating unnecessarily whenever any part of the state changed.

Performance started to degrade noticeably.
Simple actions like adding a product to the cart triggered re-renders of the entire homepage, promotional banners, and unrelated account settings components.

Debugging became slow and frustrating.
Any bug involving state required hunting through hundreds of lines in the store to understand what had triggered what.
Even small feature changes risked breaking unrelated parts of the application.

When they decided to internationalize the application later, the monolithic store became a major obstacle.
Since translation needs touched many pieces of text scattered throughout the app, and the state management was deeply entangled, adapting to multiple languages required far more rework than anticipated.

Eventually, they committed to a large, painful refactor:

Splitting state into feature-specific stores

Moving away from global subscriptions where unnecessary

Reorganizing the project into a feature-first structure

The process took months, blocked new feature work, and involved considerable technical debt payoff.

Their biggest takeaway was that **global stores must be treated with extreme caution**.
Only truly application-wide state belongs globally; feature-specific or page-

specific data should live closer to where it is used. Keeping state modular and scoped appropriately avoids tangled dependencies that can cripple an otherwise fast and lightweight application.

Another real-world case involved a startup building a mobile-focused Progressive Web App using SvelteKit.

Their team approached architecture deliberately from the beginning. They structured the project around features, each owning its routes, components, stores, services, and even tests.

They invested early in designing responsive, text-expanding layouts to handle internationalization, even before the first non-English markets launched. Forms were designed with flexible address inputs, dynamic phone number formats, and user-configurable time zones from day one.

When they later expanded into Japan, Spain, and Germany, the technical work required was minimal.
They simply plugged in new translation dictionaries, tested layouts for longer text strings, and adjusted a few marketing assets.
No major rewrites, no deep architectural changes.

The project remained under 200ms Time to Interactive even on mid-range Android devices after launching across five markets.

Their architecture also made integrating new developers straightforward. Feature folders were self-contained and could be handed off easily without needing to understand the entire application immediately.

From this success, the clear lesson was that **planning for flexibility early, even if it feels premature, unlocks incredible speed and confidence later**. You don't need to over-engineer abstractions or generalize everything too early, but respecting patterns like feature-first organization, flexible layouts, modular stores, and localized configurations ensures that growth is smooth, not painful.

One final case worth highlighting involved a small tools startup whose application suffered badly from implicit, hidden reactivity.

Their components were filled with $: reactive statements stacked on top of each other, where one variable depended on another, which depended on

189

another.

Over time, these dependencies became hard to track.

Adding new logic often led to subtle, hard-to-reproduce bugs where the UI updated incorrectly or the wrong data was displayed.

When they tried to migrate parts of the application toward newer Svelte patterns inspired by Svelte 5's runes and signals approach, the hidden coupling made it almost impossible to refactor safely.

They had to spend considerable effort untangling reactive chains manually and testing every affected behavior carefully.

Their hard-earned lesson was that **being explicit about reactive dependencies from the start** — keeping derived values close to their sources, minimizing reactive chain length, and clearly documenting intentional dependencies — saves enormous work later.

They also found that limiting component size helped.

Small components with focused reactive logic were easy to modernize and optimize.

Large components with messy reactive networks were traps for bugs and migration headaches.

Real-world case studies show that sustainable, maintainable Svelte applications are built through deliberate decisions early on:

Modular structure organized by feature, not by file type

Small, focused stores rather than sprawling global state

Clear separation of data fetching, state management, and UI rendering

Flexible layouts that anticipate internationalization and mobile diversity

Explicit, understandable reactivity to avoid hidden complexity

Svelte's design makes it easy to build beautiful applications fast — but thoughtful, disciplined architecture is what keeps those applications healthy as they grow.

By learning from the successes and struggles of real teams, you position yourself not just to ship applications quickly, but to build systems that stay robust, efficient, and joyful to work with far into the future.

Appendices

Appendix A — Quick Reference: Advanced Svelte Patterns

Understanding advanced Svelte patterns gives you the ability to write more modular, efficient, and scalable applications without unnecessary complexity.

One important pattern is **derived stores**.
Derived stores allow you to create new reactive values based on other stores without manually subscribing or wiring reactive updates.

Example:

```
import { writable, derived } from 'svelte/store';


const count = writable(0);

const doubled = derived(count, $count => $count *
2);
```
Whenever `count` changes, `doubled` recalculates automatically. This keeps reactive chains clean and avoids cluttering components with manual reactivity logic.

Another pattern that improves modularity is **slot composition**. Slots allow parent components to pass content into child components, making layouts more flexible without tightly coupling structure.

Example:

```
<!-- Modal.svelte -->
<div class="modal">
    <header><slot name="header" /></header>
    <main><slot /></main>
    <footer><slot name="footer" /></footer>
</div>
```

And then using the modal:

```
<Modal>
```

```
    <span slot="header">Modal Title</span>

    <p>This is modal content.</p>

    <button slot="footer">Close</button>

</Modal>
```

This allows components to remain generic and reusable while supporting highly customized content layouts.

Another important advanced technique is **context API usage**. When passing props through multiple levels becomes cumbersome, Svelte provides `setContext` and `getContext` to share values between components without direct prop drilling.

Setting context in a parent component:

```
import { setContext } from 'svelte';

setContext('theme', 'dark');
Getting context in a nested child:
import { getContext } from 'svelte';

const theme = getContext('theme');
```

Contexts are excellent for things like themes, authentication tokens, localization settings, and other globally relevant values.

Finally, an increasingly important pattern with Svelte 5 and beyond is **explicit reactive signals**.
Using signals (such as `signal()` from experimental APIs) provides fine-grained control over reactive updates and clarifies dependency relationships directly in code.

Understanding and practicing these patterns ensures that your Svelte codebases remain powerful without becoming hard to understand or scale.

Appendix B — Recommended Tools and Libraries

While Svelte itself provides an extremely lightweight and capable base, certain tools and libraries complement Svelte development particularly well and make professional-grade application building faster and easier.

For **state management beyond basic writable stores**, lightweight libraries like zustand or nanostores can offer patterns that scale neatly while staying close to Svelte's reactive philosophy.

When working with **routing**, SvelteKit offers a built-in filesystem-based router that covers nearly all standard needs. However, for standalone Svelte SPA (single-page application) projects, libraries like svelte-spa-router are simple and effective.

For **testing Svelte applications**, @testing-library/svelte provides tools for writing integration and unit tests that mimic real user interactions instead of focusing purely on internal implementation details.

Example Svelte component test:

```
import { render, fireEvent } from '@testing-library/svelte';

import Counter from './Counter.svelte';


test('increments count', async () => {

    const { getByText } = render(Counter);

    const button = getByText('Increment');

    await fireEvent.click(button);

    expect(getByText('Count: 1')).toBeTruthy();

});
```

For **styling**, TailwindCSS integrates well with Svelte projects, offering utility-first styling that avoids heavy custom CSS maintenance. It pairs particularly well with SvelteKit for creating fast, cleanly styled applications.

When it comes to **visualization needs**, svelte-chartjs or direct Chart.js integration can cover common charting tasks efficiently inside Svelte components.

For **form validation**, `felte` and `svelte-forms-lib` provide great Svelte-native options for building complex, reactive forms without excessive boilerplate.

For **internationalization (i18n)**, lightweight libraries like `svelte-i18n` handle multiple languages, pluralization, and localized formats efficiently inside Svelte apps without adding heavy overhead.

Lastly, for **performance analysis and optimization**, using `rollup-plugin-visualizer` during builds can help you understand bundle size and tree shaking opportunities, ensuring your application remains lean as features grow.

Choosing the right tools means aligning with Svelte's philosophy: keep things simple, efficient, and reactive, without introducing unnecessary abstraction or complexity.

Appendix C — Project Case Study: Architecting a Scalable SvelteKit App

Scaling a modern web application is about much more than adding new features over time.
It requires a careful balance between project structure, state management, routing, performance optimization, and developer experience.
Getting these foundations right at the beginning determines whether a project can grow smoothly or whether it accumulates technical debt that eventually slows development.

In this case study, we will walk through how a real production SvelteKit application was designed from the ground up with **scalability**, **maintainability**, and **performance** as core goals.

When this project began, the primary goal was to build a business dashboard application for managing user accounts, billing, notifications, analytics, and system   settings.
The team knew that while the initial scope was small, future expansions were guaranteed, including internationalization, mobile optimization, and the addition of real-time features.

Folder Structure and Feature Organization

The team chose to organize the project around **features** instead of technical types.
Instead of placing all components in one folder and all stores in another, each feature had its own folder containing everything it needed.

Their structure looked like this:

```
src/

  features/

    auth/

      LoginForm.svelte

      authStore.js

      authService.js

    billing/

      BillingPage.svelte

      billingStore.js

      billingService.js

    dashboard/

      DashboardHome.svelte

      dashboardStore.js

      dashboardService.js

  components/

    Navbar.svelte

    Sidebar.svelte

    Modal.svelte

  lib/
```

```
   utils/

      dateFormat.js

      apiClient.js

  stores/

     globalStore.js
```

Each **feature folder** contained:

UI components specific to that feature

Localized stores for managing feature state

Services responsible for API communication

Any helper utilities used primarily within that feature

This structure allowed teams working on different features to operate independently.
It also kept changes tightly scoped and reduced the risk of breaking unrelated parts of the application.

Global components and utilities lived separately in `components/` and `lib/`, ensuring a clean distinction between project-wide assets and feature-specific logic.

State Management Strategy

Global state was kept minimal and deliberate.
Only data that needed to be shared across features — such as user session data, application theme settings, and notification counts — were stored globally using a `globalStore.js`.

For example, the global user store:

```
// src/stores/globalStore.js
import { writable } from 'svelte/store';

export const user = writable(null);

export function login(userData) {
```

```
        user.set(userData);
}

export function logout() {
        user.set(null);
}
```

Feature-specific state, such as billing history or dashboard analytics, lived inside feature folders using local stores.

Keeping most state local reduced unintended reactivity and made the application easier to test, debug, and extend without unnecessary global complexity.

Routing and Layouts

The application took full advantage of SvelteKit's filesystem-based routing.

Routes were structured to match feature areas naturally:

```
src/routes/

   login/+page.svelte

   dashboard/+layout.svelte

   dashboard/+page.svelte

   dashboard/analytics/+page.svelte

   billing/+page.svelte
```

The `+layout.svelte` for `/dashboard` provided shared components like the sidebar, top navigation, and base page styling.

Each feature had its own child routes underneath, allowing page-specific metadata, page titles, and even route guards (checking user authentication before allowing access).

This clean routing structure made it easy to build new feature areas without worrying about breaking existing navigation or layout behavior.

Data Fetching and API Services

Rather than scattering API calls throughout components, the team centralized API interaction inside service modules.

Example billing service:

```
// src/features/billing/billingService.js
import { apiClient } from
'$lib/utils/apiClient.js';

export async function fetchInvoices() {
    const response = await
apiClient.get('/invoices');
    if (!response.ok) {
        throw new Error('Failed to fetch
invoices');
    }
    return response.json();
}
```

Components then imported service functions:

```
<script>
    import { fetchInvoices } from
'$features/billing/billingService.js';
    import { onMount } from 'svelte';
    let invoices = [];

    onMount(async () => {
        invoices = await fetchInvoices();
    });
</script>
```

This separation kept components simple and focused only on UI logic, improving readability and testability.

Styling Strategy

The team used TailwindCSS integrated with SvelteKit for consistent, utility-first styling.

To avoid bloated CSS output, they configured Tailwind's purge settings carefully:

```
// tailwind.config.js
```

```
module.exports = {
    content: ['./src/**/*.{html,js,svelte,ts}'],
    theme: {
        extend: {},
    },
    plugins: [],
};
```

Using utility classes directly in Svelte components minimized custom CSS and kept bundle sizes small.

Performance Considerations

The team used several performance practices consistently:

Lazy loading components when appropriate using dynamic imports

Prefetching critical data during page navigation with SvelteKit's `load` functions

Code splitting large modules automatically by relying on SvelteKit's routing and build system

Bundle size analysis using `rollup-plugin-visualizer` during production builds to catch oversized dependencies early

Combined, these practices allowed the application to maintain fast load times even as new features were added.

First Contentful Paint consistently measured under 1 second on mobile devices across global test markets.

Internationalization Support

From the beginning, the team planned for multiple languages.

They used `svelte-i18n`, setting up a simple translation store with JSON dictionaries for English, Spanish, and French.

At runtime, users could switch languages dynamically without needing a full page reload.

Key translation usage:

```
<script>
    import { t } from 'svelte-i18n';
</script>

<h1>{$t('dashboard.welcome')}</h1>
```

This decision made it easy to launch into new markets with minimal friction.

Testing and Quality Assurance

Testing was integrated early using `@testing-library/svelte` for component testing and Playwright for end-to-end browser testing.

An example component test for login form validation:

```
import { render, fireEvent } from '@testing-library/svelte';
import LoginForm from './LoginForm.svelte';

test('shows error when submitting empty form',
async () => {
    const { getByText, getByLabelText } =
render(LoginForm);

    await fireEvent.click(getByText('Login'));

    expect(getByText('Username is
required')).toBeTruthy();
    expect(getByText('Password is
required')).toBeTruthy();
});
```

Automated tests caught regressions early and made upgrades to SvelteKit or third-party libraries safer and faster.

Architecting a scalable SvelteKit application requires thoughtful decisions in project organization, state management, routing, data fetching, styling, and testing.

By structuring by feature, isolating concerns, using service layers, planning for global needs, and adopting modern tooling from the beginning, the team in this case study built an application that remained fast, reliable, and maintainable even as it expanded to serve more users, more features, and new markets.

Their success came not from complicated abstractions, but from applying simple, consistent, forward-looking principles professionally and rigorously.

By learning from this practical case study, you now have a clear blueprint for building SvelteKit applications that are not only impressive today, but sustainable and adaptable far into the future.